PUBLISHED IN JUNE 2024

THE TITLE, STYLE OF MAKE-UP AND CONTENTS OF THIS
ALMANACK ARE STRICTLY COPYRIGHT

Foulsham's Original
OLD MOORE'S ALMANACK

1697   THE ORIGINAL COPYRIGHT EDITION   **2025**

2025 – The Digital Winds Will Blow

It's clear: there will be stormy seas for the world in 2025. Fortunately, the UK is a tough little boat that will sail faster than most others. We will have more direction in our government and be more united in resolving our problems.

America is my biggest concern. In difficult times, it does not have our unity. The best of America will still be the best of the world, but the federal government will continue to serve corporate interests instead of its electorate and will continue to be referred to as corrupt. It is American strength that has maintained world stability. It has done so by controlling international dollar trading and by enforcing its dollar monopoly over oil, through the Petrodollar. But in 2025, the dollar will lose too much value and I expect its controls to be broken. I expect oil producers to agree to trade directly using local currencies backed by gold or Bitcoin. This will pose a significant threat to world order as we have known it.

The world, too, must expect to be drawn into this change. Bitcoin is what makes this attack possible, and it will continue to increase in strength throughout the year. It seems likely to become a preferred alternative to the security of a weakening dollar.

At home, we will begin to address the human issues that need to be corrected and resolved. We all want to see profound changes to our political and social fabric. Everyone wants to believe our politicians and civil servants. Everyone wants more truth. There will be a strong desire for a return to honest, responsible statesmanship.

I'm afraid that we will be disappointed. I expect to see yet more messy politicking designed to obscure the truth. No matter how pioneering our policies appear, I still expect a healthy dose of scepticisms about political honesty. The reassuring statements coming from

© 2024 by OLD MOORE PUBLICATIONS
Published under Annual Licence by W. Foulsham & Co. Ltd
Printed and bound by CPI Group (UK) Ltd, Croydon, CR0 4YY
News trade distribution by Seymour 020 7429 4000

Tel: (01628) 400600
The Old Barrel Store,
Drayman's Lane,
Marlow, Bucks SL7 2FF

A look ahead to events in 2025

our civil service will continue to contain credibility gaps. Unhappily, they will likely become even worse. Public trust in the civil service will become embarrassingly low. Righteous causes will continue to engage British politics, but there will need to be a dose of realism for the outcomes to be acceptable. A move towards more individualism will begin to emerge. This year will see a realisation that we are without the social support we hoped for. To get things done, being outspoken will become very on trend during 2025.

Three major planetary influences will be important to us in the year. *Compassionate* Saturn moves into *strong-minded* Aries alongside *impressionable* Neptune, while *revolutionary* Uranus moves into Gemini, the sign of intelligence.

In our context, a better alternative word to use for 'communication' is 'intelligence'. This is at the heart of the hottest topic of the year: **A**rtificial **I**ntelligence. AI will save lives and move mankind in amazing directions. The government will need to upgrade its hardware and software, and these new capabilities should speed up the delivery of social justice and better public services. At long last, you may think. Medical science will experience explosive enhancements, ushering in a new era of turbo-charged health discoveries and new health delivery methods. I will be searching for advancements, such as artificial limbs controlled by brain power.

Through Gemini, the influencer of vehicles and highways, we will witness the first Full-Self-Drive Car, with safety stats surpassing 100%! This staggering break-through is the product of Video-Artificial-Intelligence. It will prove much safer than human driving and continue to improve every year as it learns yet more from its experience. Full-Self-Drive will be a game-changer for Tesla, the only company capable of delivering the software that makes it possible.

I anticipate a tsunami of digital breakthroughs, capable of radically changing the world. 2025 will offer our first glimpse of astonishing new tools. We are entering another Industrial Revolution that will create a brighter future in the workplace.

The prevailing influences over the UK will be similar to those that brought positive changes for Tony Blair in 1997. However, the presence of Neptune alongside the influential Aries suggests that we may be taking risks on behalf of others. During the summer, unexpected world events will force us to make difficult decisions. Expect surprising changes and a tough approach. Government agencies will face challenges on behalf of the nation and the world. Their determination to manage these circumstances will come as a surprise when compared with our recent experiences.

Throughout 2025, we will grow weary of war and seek solutions. Closures may be found, as the Saturn–Neptune conjunction often brings about changes from oppressive conditions. There is much to hope for in 2025. The planetary influences encourage us all to seek and find forgiveness. The overview prompts us to let go of past angers. In fact, the theme of my year is precisely that – letting bygones be bygones. I wish you well in doing this for yourself, dear reader.

Dr Francis Moore, September 2023

0906 822 9723: *ring Old Moore now* – for the most authentic personal phone horoscope ever made available

Then just tap in your own birth date ... and benefit from the wisdom of the centuries

The uncanny foresight of Britain's No 1 astrologer – focused directly on your own individual birth-chart

Unique personalised reading

There's never been a better way to exploit your personal horoscope opportunities.

Old Moore now has a massive new computer and can produce a personal forecast based on the actual day of your birth. No other astro phone advice service can produce this level of accuracy.

Any day of the week, Old Moore can update you on the planetary influences which surround you and point up the opportunities which will be open to you.

Unique record of prediction

The principles of astro interpretation laid down by Old Moore have proved amazingly reliable and accurate. That's how the Almanack continues to astound the world, year after year. And that's how Old Moore can analyse your own personal world.

PS: phone today and see what you should be looking out for.

Meet Old Moore any day

For just 60p per minute you can hear this authoritative overview of your life, work and happiness. Not the usual 'fortune-telling' patter. But enlightened insights into how best to exploit the day and the ***moment***.

Remember, unlike any other phone astrologer, Old Moore will ask you for the ***day, month and year*** of your birth, to give you the most individual advice and predictions ever possible.

So touch hands with the immortal Old Moore. Ring this number and get a truly personalised forecast, from the world's most acclaimed astrologer.

0906 822 9723

Calls cost 60p per minute at all times.
(Charges may be higher for payphones and non-BT networks).
Complaints & Service Provider (ATS): 0844 836 9769

2025 – World Preview

UNITED KINGDOM AND WORLD ECONOMY

A strong astrological configuration on the New York Stock exchange could depress markets in 2025, and there is geopolitical uncertainty as international supply chains are affected. However, with energetic Sun and Mars affecting the FTSE 250 'birth chart', shares in Britain should remain generally buoyant and investors may even show themselves to be overconfident. All the same there is a possibility that UK economic growth overall will be slow with a reduction in interest rates.

January is likely to see a challenging start in Westminster with unexpected obstacles in view as the government is rebuffed on a foreign policy matter. In February, Britain may be pursuing UK–US trade agreements and trying to fix problems by looking back to the past and retrying what some will see as redundant policies. All the same, we can expect the solar eclipse in Aries (late March) to shake things up and force the government to incorporate new thinking. Younger Members of Parliament may be coming to the fore.

In summer there may be a turn-around, with progressive Jupiter involved in four major aspects. Confidence should be high in the government in July, with new reforms and successful investments, and with even a boost for the property market and affordable housing. A second solar eclipse occurs on 21 September in Virgo, which may point to a crisis or – equally a significant breakthrough in how the NHS is to be run. In November, the Labour leadership could be rooting out dissent from disgruntled back benchers, who may be protesting the lack of democratic spirit.

UNITED STATES

The inauguration of the new President is set for 20 January 2025 and the chart for this day shows a powerful configuration that suggests one of the most controversial, even surprising, presidencies ever. One forecast chart with Venus–Saturn conjoined suggests that progressivism and liberal values may actually be unpopular, and traditional, conservative attitudes preferred. The position of Venus at the time of the inauguration does appear to support the possibility of the sitting President being removed. It will be a close-run thing.

Economically, GDP will improve in 2025, but disparity in income will reach its highest peak. March may see a major period of confusion or scandal in the corridors of power, while April is likely to see US states adopting new rules to combat gerrymandering as a result of AI technologies that provide more impartial and competitive voting systems. In July or September, competition in the tech wars between the USA and China could dominate the news. By October, the President will be filled with grandiose ideas and the USA is in a period of self-confidence, boosting US businesses and exports.

EUROPE/GERMANY

The German Bundestag election will probably be held in Autumn 2025. Astrological determinators show the Christian Democrats on course to make a comeback, whilst the approval rating for Olaf Scholz and his SDP may continue to drop. Dissatisfaction among the German people over inflated prices and a stalling economy will be the cause. The forecast chart up to October 2025 suggests conciliation, harmony and finding solutions, and an aspect between Venus, Mars and Saturn indicates safe handling of the economy and effective government.

From October 2025, an election win by the Christian Democrats may be welcomed but under the Saturn–Neptune conjunction the new coalition government may be severely criticised for seeming incompetent or being too soft. With reckless Uranus also prominent, certain political alliances made by Germany could prove unstable, and with vague Neptune to the fore, too much ground will be given in any serious deal-making. Despite the unexciting economic picture in Germany, inflation may be falling in the European Central Bank – possibly faster than most pundits would expect.

ISRAEL

The 2025 predictive chart depicts Israel stubbornly going its own way in spite of outside criticism. One main forecast chart shows popular Venus in Netanyahu's 'career' house that may scotch any talk of early elections as the effects of the war with Hamas continue to play out. Enabling Jupiter may be helping to keep Netanyahu in power. This may not be what many in the world wants to hear but Western powers have been, so far, broadly supportive of Israel's right to defend itself. As we reach June or July 2025, stern intervention by the USA may lead to the basis for future, peaceful political arrangements.

RUSSIA/CHINA

Financial stresses in Russia's chart suggest it could be time to alter course in 2025 – one astrological indicator shows international trade under severe pressure. Ukraine may cede some territory while using a 'hold and build' tactic for 2025 – although indications from forecast charts are that Putin may eventually want to seek some kind of settlement in the middle part of the year, while appearing not to have lost. The worst-case scenario for Ukraine would be an isolationist position in US foreign policy – and if Trump were to take the Presidency, the planets suggest this is a likely outcome.

In early 2025, Russia will move to strengthen its alliance with China which will be flexing its muscles in a big way. This eases and facilitates China's grand designs, so diplomatic missions by Western powers should be top of the agenda. Possible flashpoints occur in July and October when China may have finished building a nuclear-powered aircraft carrier.

Sophie, Duchess of Edinburgh

© Mick Atkins/Shutterstock

It may, perhaps, be true to say that at one time, she could have been described as one of the 'dark horses' of the Royal Family – but no more. Her public role has become ever more prominent – pivotal even – as she has stepped into the breach left by King Charles's illness, and so today she is more likely to be dubbed the Royal Family's 'secret weapon'. As we will see, this kind of efficient, leave-it-to-me approach won't surprise astrologers, nor would her involvement in various worthy causes, such as serving lunch to Ukrainian refugees or making trips to Colombia to show support for female survivors of violence. She has also established the Women's Network Forum, supporting victims of exploitation. These causes aren't simply PR photo-ops either, which may be why the public have come to like and respect her. She was even said to be the late Queen's 'favourite daughter-in-law', a compliment she repaid by calling the Queen 'mama'! All in all, she now has the unofficial role of Public Relations Officer for the Royal Family, the 'Firm', if only because she understands that role so well. Let's find out why and look at her birth chart.

The former Sophie Rhys-Jones, now Sophie, Duchess of Edinburgh, was born on 20 January 1965 in Oxford. This makes her a kind-hearted, humanitarian Sun Aquarian with the Moon in hardworking and capable Virgo. The unverified birth time we have of 12.46 pm gives Gemini rising; however, Old Moore suggests that a slightly later time of about 2.00 pm (giving Cancer rising) is more in keeping with what we know of Sophie. It's been said that she's very warm, down-to-earth and approachable and great with children, with a natural flair for communication 'because she can empathise as well as sympathise. She has that compassion, which is so lovely'. This is exactly what you'd expect of a Sun Aquarian (the sign of a 'people person') with homely, maternal, sensitive Cancer on the ascendant.

Sophie's Moon (feelings) is conjunct rebellious Uranus and intense Pluto in judgemental, analytical Virgo so, inwardly, she has some balancing to do. It's an aspect indicating highly personal (even inflexible) ideas and very strong opinions that aren't about to change any time soon. These she has learned simply to keep to herself, knowing well the importance of maintaining the appropriate public face. Venus (harmony) and Mercury (communication) in Capricorn produce a keen sense of tradition, with both planets in the seventh house of relationships and diplomacy and 'correct' behaviour. These planetary positions would have made her an ideal ambassador when she co-owned

The Royal Family's 'secret weapon'?

the firm RJH Public Relations. She's thus known as a clever diplomat who can pour oil on any troubled waters among the Royals, of which there have been several.

Let us turn now to her highly successful partnership with Edward, the Duke of Edinburgh (born 10 March 1964 at 8.20 pm). This is the only marriage of the late Queen's children not to be sundered by divorce. Sophie met Edward during her four-year stint at Capital Radio, where she worked in the press department. Married on 19 June 1999, the couple have two children, Lady Louise Windsor and James, Earl of Wessex, and are often regarded as the archetypal perfect pair. But does the astrology bear this out? The Synastry technique, which examines how one partner's planets contact the other partner's, shows her Moon conjunct his Pluto, and opposite his Mars. This can prove very intense and not a little explosive but can also be a big emotional bond.

Turning to the Composite chart, a kind of x-ray of a relationship, we see the 'love planet' Venus, Saturn (tradition) and Sun (identity) in the seventh house of marriage, signifying a stress on *facing the world as a unit*, a genuine couple. High-minded Jupiter is also involved, so there is honesty and integrity in the relationship. Venus in the seventh signifies harmony, shared feelings and emotions, to the point where neither really likes to disagree with the other. It's no wonder, then, that one body language expert has commented how Sophie and Edward's physical gestures, when in public, so often mirror each other. This 'mirroring' happens when people are in harmony or on the same page as each other. Taskmaster Saturn is also in the seventh house, meaning the partners are bound to each other not simply through affection but by duty and obligation.

Usually undertaking over 200 engagements in a year as patron of over 70 charities, Sophie's workload may increase further in 2025. One predictive chart for 2025 shows Venus and Saturn conjunct ('home' in the fourth house), with its implications of 'minding the store' with family duties and responsibilities – hence extra Royal engagements and charity work. January could be a tough month of hard work, when health matters also come into focus. Sophie may feel strongly that there's too little time for recreational matters, especially in March to the end of April when freedom-demanding Uranus is prominent. And with responsible Saturn at large in June, it's a time to slow down and keep duties to a minimum – if that's possible.

However, the second half of the year is different as enabling, optimistic Jupiter is to the fore during the rest of June. Astrologically, a new personal cycle begins for Sophie and an individual project close to her heart may begin. It may even represent a turning point of sorts, where unsought professional assistance will lighten her load considerably. A new personal friendship may also begin, and there are high-points in her relationship with Edward in July and August – periods of great contentment. Despite the extra workload, the Duchess will demand the right to be herself and will have the opportunity for this in 2025. She may also assume the limelight as never before: a 'dark horse' no longer!

Michael McIntyre

© Rich Gold/Alamy Stock Photo

It seems almost paradoxical for someone of Michael McIntyre's popularity and standing to be an individual who, from a personal point of view, is often lacking in self-confidence and who probably remains perpetually surprised by his amazing success – but such is the legacy of the birth chart he possesses.

Michael was born on 21 February 1976 in Merton, south London. This, first and foremost, gives him a Sun placed in Pisces, undoubtedly the most sensitive of all the zodiac signs. Add to this the Moon in Scorpio, which, like Pisces, is a Water sign and it is obvious from the start that this is an individual who thinks deeply and who works from a strong, spiritual base. Michael often hides these qualities well, mainly thanks to the fact that the zodiac sign of Virgo was rising at the time of his birth – which makes him industrious and gives him a harder edge than do his Sun and Moon. This strong Virgo quality offers direction and a natural creativity that is turned to practical use.

Michael McIntyre has a strong work ethic, good physical resilience (though he can become exhausted and needs periods of recuperation) and he has particularly strong instincts when it comes to seeing the potential of the 'next idea', many of which crowd his fertile imagination perpetually. Mars contacting Neptune in his chart allows Michael to lock into people immediately and he is immensely likeable – even though his circle of personal friends may not be large and a lot of the contacts he makes are likely to be casual and not lasting.

Michael McIntyre, whose career has been consistent and successful for some time is best known these days for his Saturday night television appearances, but these give impetus to the part of his career which is likely to be more personally stimulating to a person with Mercury and Venus both in Aquarius – his stand-up shows. He fills stadiums and delights more fans than just about any comedian from the past or present. This aspect of Michael McIntyre's career is likely to continue, but we may see him utilising his television potential in a different way by taking on dramatic roles, whilst the power of his Virgo ascendant is so strong that he may also enter yet another career, this time as a writer. Whatever direction he chooses, we certainly have not yet seen the untapped potential of this most talented individual.

Despite the continued tours and possibly another blockbuster Saturday night extravaganza, what is clear is that Michael needs periods of quiet reflection if he is not to exhaust himself to an extent that might mean a long period out of the spotlight and away from his adoring public. Nevertheless, with a sensible balance, the Michael McIntyre phenomenon is set to run and run.

Vladimir Putin

© SERGEY BOBYLEV/SPUTNIK/KREMLIN POOL/EPA-EFE/Shutterstock

One of the more controversial figures on the world stage, Vladimir Putin, was again victorious in Russia's 2024 presidential elections, succeeding with 88% of the vote. Regular readers of *Old Moore* will know that the astrological indicators for his leadership point to this longevity. Now the world holds its breath. As long as Putin remains in power, pundits fear that the war on Ukraine will continue, possibly with even grander designs. There is little to stop him continuing in this vein for years. While the Russian economy has its weaknesses, it's not falling apart. What next, then?

Putin was born in Saint Petersburg, then known as Leningrad, on 7 October 1952 at 9.30 am. He is a Sun Libran, with several other key planets in his birth chart's twelfth house – the area of secrecy and hidden motives. It's a heavy chart with serious, passionate Scorpio rising, extremely defensive and driven by the need for control; the same thing is seen again with Pluto (power) conjunct MC (profession). Mercury (communication) is also conjoined conservative Saturn, making him stubborn in his opinions. This planetary configuration gives him resilience and aids him in his bid for total power, helping ensure rivals don't stand a chance. A lighter note is struck by Moon in airy, curious in Gemini which excels at political sleight-of-hand. Preferring the shadows, he will not enjoy the media spotlight created by the Ukraine invasion.

The key astrological note in 2025 is grandiose Jupiter sensitively placed on a predictive chart, helping to smooth his path. Relations between the West and Russia will be at their lowest level ever this year, and since the main Western goal is containing an expansionist Russia, this may prove difficult, given that Jupiter's archetypal principle is one of expansion! However, there is another factor at play – manipulative Pluto on the Midheaven, posing a danger when handling such great power. Could Putin make a misstep in 2025? He could.

In either March or June, the upgrading of Russia's nuclear arsenal may be in the news, and the testing of missiles may also resume. These months are also tense from a political perspective – the right time for enemies at home to strike, although any internal putsch to remove him from power may be premature. The current sanctions regime may be tightened in April; such pressure may even cause a re-think over war strategies.

However, if Putin overcomes opposition at home by June, then, astrologically speaking, he may have a free hand to pursue his aims, perhaps enacting more stringent measures against abortion. Most astrological indications show Putin with the green light, with support, even, from China, so it's just as well that Western unity is likely to remain strong during 2025.

What drives the man behind Tesla?

Elon Musk

© Jeffrey Mayer/Alamy Stock Photo

Entrepreneur Elon Musk, co-founder of PayPal and Tesla, is no stranger to controversy. Immediately after he'd acquired social media site Twitter for $44 billion in 2022, there were, let's say, serious concerns following the name change to X, and the decision to reinstate ex-US president Donald Trump's account. Then there were racist and antisemitic tweets, which increased following Musk's takeover, some of them self-authored. What is it, then, that drives him?

He was born Elon Reeve Musk on 28 June 1971 at 7.30 am, in Pretoria, South Africa, which gives him Sun (self/individuality) and ascendant (identity/physicality) in emotional Cancer, and the Moon (feelings) in analytical Virgo. Cancer is the sign to note here – self-protective and sentimental. The Sun is also in the twelfth house, the traditional 'house of self-undoing' where one can be one's own worst enemy. His adversarial relationship with the press and thin skin when criticised have been observed.

This is all very Cancerian, but the relationship with his father has also been publicly problematic and Musk has said: 'He's good at making life miserable'. The father issues are indicated by a Moon–Saturn configuration, leaving him very defensive emotionally, and where self-control is a big thing. The Sun's contact with expansive Jupiter and dreamy Neptune stimulates his imagination but also gives him an unrealistic self-image – people see him very differently from how he sees himself.

Even so, with quickening Uranus in a harsh aspect to Mercury (the mind) he has a massive appetite for learning and needs to know everything instantly. Impatient with ideas, he's also a multi-tasker with nervous energy and impatience. Uranus's influence makes Elon want to go against the grain *just for the sake of being different*. Libertarian free-speech is everything to him, but often leads him to cause offence. And there's an inconsistency, too: one biographer perceptively described him as 'mercurial', citing his 'variable moods'. Precisely – a sensitive, moody Cancerian with Mercury on the ascendant!

So, what does 2025 hold? Up until June, with combative Mars prominent, we may hear more outspoken gaffes and indiscretions. After his birthday in June though, a new astrological configuration operates when we'll see a more conciliatory individual, reaching out to others. Summer (especially July) will prove his most favourable period for business, although new romance may also be in the offing in April. 2025 is the year when lucky Jupiter occupies his Sun sign: new relationships and opportunities to advance come to the fore, yet in some instances he'll be forging ahead *against* the odds, perhaps creating unnecessary problems as he goes. Astrologically, he wouldn't have it any other way.

The Future Beckons – Uranus into Gemini, Neptune into Aries for 2025

Two major planetary ingresses occur in 2025 when Uranus moves into Gemini and Neptune enters Aries; the effects of these astrological events will be felt over the next fourteen years.

URANUS INTO GEMINI

Often associated with disruption, revolt and unwelcome change, Uranus is the archetypal rebel or freedom fighter, but he's also the creative innovator, or the lightning that vivifies and animates whatever he touches. Uranus works on a collective level, too; that is, *impersonally* – often through drastic change of some kind, especially when the old order has become repressive.

Uranus in Gemini is going to influence specifically *Geminian* issues – information (and IT), education, communication (in all its forms), and transport. During its last time there, in the 1940s, the transistor, a key electronic component, was invented. So was ENIAC, the first digital computer and the aqua lung – Gemini rules breathing! There were significant advancements in the field of prosthetics – Gemini rules the limbs also.

And so, Uranus is present when there's real technological breakthrough, and it's lately revolutionised our retail experiences with cashless purchases as it transits Taurus, ruler of resources, shopping and consumerism. In 2018, Amazon piloted a 'checkout-free corner shop' scheme: where sensors and trackers log purchases digitally without the need for a checkout. If Uranus in Taurus is transforming e-commerce, with Uranus in Gemini, *urbanisation* will become a bigger trend: major high street brands will be replaced by cottage industries and small co-operatives helping to recover a sense of community. Gemini rules neighbours, and futurologists have predicted how – by 2025 – small-scale, on-demand, *locally* produced or manufactured goods will gain more popularity as unreliable supply chains across the world are affected. In other words, you won't have to wait as long for your order!

With Uranus in Gemini in 2025, we can also expect more innovative use of drones, especially in the delivery of mail and parcels. Smart cars will get even smarter, and driverless vehicles are likely to get the green light in the UK as a result of the positive Uranus–Pluto configuration in September–October. The old story of robots replacing humans may also surface and there will be moves to replace some aspects of traditional school or college education with online learning, as the obsession with AI and its powers increases. In the words of one AI enthusiast, digital apps can alone be used to 'deliver knowledge' tailored to an individual student. Plus, art and graphic design can now be facilitated by intelligent robots that carry out voice commands. Where this leaves human teachers and illustrators, we can but speculate. In science, one innovation may be new technologies that prolong life as never before. Then again, a new 'me decade' (with Neptune in Aries) may be on its way ...

NEPTUNE INTO ARIES

The other major ingress in 2025 is when Aries plays host to Neptune, a planet symbolising our sense of spirituality, our search for that other realm, for meaning and oneness with all of life. Or perhaps for temporary escapism. Collectively, Neptune shows (sign-wise) what humans are gravitating towards in the prevailing culture, or simply what's in fashion – certain collective tastes and values colour the Zeitgeist according to which sign Neptune is currently occupying. Of late, we've had Neptune moving through Pisces, since 2012.

Blurring or transcending traditional boundaries is typically Neptunian, and Pisces is the sign of everyday humanity. This lies behind the rise of transgender and non-binary gender identities. But what changes will occur as Neptune moves into Aries in 2025? Aries is a 'masculine' sign, the archetypal, independent 'hero' ready to win the day. With Neptune here there will be debates about what it means to be male in a time of gender fluidity. Marriage may dwindle in keeping with the fashion for individuality and independence. The 1970s were known as the 'me decade' when it seemed the *self*, and our exploration of it through pop psychologies, became a veritable cult. Such obsessions may reoccur.

I should also mention the Saturn–Neptune conjunction in Aries which occurs in June, July and August 2025. Here we have the orthodox reality-based (Saturn) meeting its spiritual, faith-based opposite (Neptune) – cosmically aligned, but the two planets couldn't be more different. This Saturn–Neptune conjunction will probably further the divisiveness we've recently seen in politics and public discourse, particularly on-line forums, with one side devoted to facts (Saturn) and the other to wild beliefs and conspiracies (Neptune). A major culture war was enacted in the UK around the same time that Trump was readying for his presidential campaign in 2016, and on 23 June that year we had the Brexit referendum, co-inciding with a harsh Saturn–Neptune alignment). The conduct of the Leave and Remain campaigns was based not on informed comment but scare stories about the terrible consequences were one to vote the 'wrong way'.

With Neptune in Pisces we've been adrift in a sea of incompatible narratives purported by politicians and the media about what's really real and which authority to believe. Neptune in Aries will make many issues much, much clearer, with the deceivers and propagandists far better exposed – especially in politics. It's going to be a kind of awakening; Aries is a sign of honesty and unambiguous truth. With the addition of the Saturn–Neptune conjunction in mid-2025, former, long-standing injustices or grievances may be finally corrected, but it won't be a time for revenge; rather, one for compassion, even forgiveness. Neptune in Aries is broadly about righteous causes (Neptunian sympathy combined with the dragon-slaying qualities of Aries) and we may even see the emergence of a new, dynamic, highly popular figurehead from the spiritual/self-help or political sphere who embodies this altruistic crusade. This may see the rise of a leader to whom many will want to rally.

What do the stars say for this American superstar?

Taylor Swift

© Erik Pendzich/Alamy Stock Photo

Taylor Swift was born on 13 December 1989 at 05.17 in Reading, Pennsylvania. With a few lucky breaks but mainly thanks to hard work, good health and masses of talent she has become one of the most famous people on the planet and is a billionaire. Taylor is predominantly a singer and songwriter, but her talents seem without limit and she has remained successfully in the public eye for longer than many performers could hope for.

Taylor Swift's success is assisted by her strong Sun in Sagittarius, which heads a collection of planets spread across the sign of Capricorn and with Scorpio on the ascendant at the time she was born. Her Sun was approaching the ascendant at her birth, meaning she could hardly have inherited a better astrological profile. Sagittarius gives her adaptability, excellent communication skills and the necessary savvy to guide her own ship in life. Scorpio brings the sensitivity necessary, not only to write all the songs that have made her famous, but the general balance of her chart makes her an entrepreneur *par excellence*.

Taylor has a vast fan base, which only seems to grow as the years pass and part of the reason for this, in addition to the fact that people simply love her music, is the fact that she has the Moon in Cancer, which naturally attracts others and establishes an instant bond between her and the 'Swifties' who follow her.

Mercury in Capricorn acts as a slight brake to the position of what could otherwise be a 'runaway' Sagittarian Sun and brings an instinctive depth to her song-writing, while also limiting the number of chances she is inclined to take in life. All in all, this is the astrological profile of a careful, perhaps even calculating, individual, with good common sense and an above average intelligence.

As is the case in any life, that of Taylor Swift has not been without its stumbling blocks, though these never seem to have influenced her career path. The adaptability of Sagittarius and the strength of her outer planets have taken her from one genre of music to another in a seamless flow that her fans have found easy to follow. However, it might be suggested that Taylor's personal life has not been too settled or stable because she has had a number of different romantic attachments and up to now has shown no inclination to fix on a lifetime relationship. Not that this is inevitably seen by Taylor herself as an impediment. With Venus in Aquarius, a Scorpio ascendant and that Sagittarian Sun it is quite possible that the situation is not only under control but is everything that she wishes it to be. The road ahead looks clear and bright for Taylor Swift and even more new possibilities await her.

Your 2025 Birthday Guide

By working with the major astrological influences, you can take control and give your life a better focus. These personal guides show you how to make the most of the positive times and also indicate which days need to be handled with care.

ARIES BORN PEOPLE
Birthdays: 21 March to 20 April inclusive
Planet: Mars. Birthstone: Diamond. Lucky day: Tuesday

Keynote for the Year: *The past really is something to learn from as you grow this year, yet your most rewarding times may come through new family developments.*

JANUARY: MAIN TRENDS: 3–4 Organisation and practicality are your watchwords as the year begins and you're driven to manage and control situations, but you might find that going with the flow could work better. **15–16** You may encounter some opposition at work, and you may need to recognise certain limitations. **20–21** A socially inspiring time when you should enjoy companionship and teamwork. **KEY DATES: HIGHS 6–7** Aim high now as trends bring you an uncanny ability to get your own way. **LOWS 19–21** Prepare for disagreements and difficulties at work arising from confusion, especially in relation to schedules.

FEBRUARY: MAIN TRENDS: 1–2 Trends see you initiating good ideas and getting them underway, whether personally or professionally. **7–9** Take any opportunity to break with everyday routine; your personality sparkles with fun and good humour which bodes well for your social life. **20–21** A great time to begin a new partnership, whether business or pleasure. Your diplomatic skills will also come in handy. **KEY DATES: HIGHS 3–4** The monthly high sees you feeling your best, enjoying life and fulfilling your objectives. **LOWS 15–17** Slow down and try to get some rest now, Aries.

MARCH: MAIN TRENDS: 14–15 At work new powers of leadership may boost your confidence in the way ahead. **16–17** Accept some friendly assistance and work should become easier and mundane routine less boring. **20–21** With the Sun now in your sign your ideas are creative and effective. Multi-tasking and versatility are also major strengths. **KEY DATES: HIGHS 1–2; 29–30** A planetary high point when you're up to any challenge and way ahead of everyone. **LOWS 15–16** Consider this period as time for a break between activities.

APRIL: MAIN TRENDS: 2–4 You're popular and making a dynamic impact on others, something that loved ones find especially attractive. **10–11** Prepare for challenges at work and for progress to slow – hang back with big decisions. **21–22** A new financial proposition may be promising if you build on a profitable start. **KEY DATES: HIGHS 25–26** Tempt fate a little during the monthly high, and don't be afraid to run ahead of the pack. **LOWS 11–13** Accept any small instability now with good grace and go with the flow.

MAY: MAIN TRENDS: 1–2 The planet of communication is in your sign and trends suggest you will be busy socially, so look out for worthwhile information in your meetings. **3–5** An enjoyable period of closeness with a partner or fun social activities. **20–21** Decisiveness and quick thinking are now your forte; snap decisions could work out well. But remember to consider plans on your long-term agenda. **KEY DATES: HIGHS 23–24** Trends bring you more control over things at work – use this influence to your advantage. **LOWS 8–10** Take care of essential duties and seek help if needed, then it's time for a rest.

Aries: plan ahead for your best times

JUNE: MAIN TRENDS: 3–4 Domestic chores or difficulties may restrict your ability to seek excitement elsewhere. Bide your time and be fair. **15–16** As long as you have plenty of mental stimulation, daily life should provide lots to make you feel happy and fulfilled. **21–22** The spirit of nostalgia is stronger than usual now and may prove especially favourable for a family reunion. **KEY DATES: HIGHS 19–20** As your confidence in your own ability grows, now is the time to push ahead faster. **LOWS 5–6** Take things as easily as possible during this planetary lull.

JULY: MAIN TRENDS: 4–5 Talks with loved ones now could reveal significant information, perhaps regarding an imminent decision. **8–9** An insatiable appetite for new things may keep you on the go, whether this is in travel, making connections or just broadening your thinking. **21–22** Prepare for increased responsibility at work, although trends suggest this is a good time to ask a favour from those in authority. **KEY DATES: HIGHS 16–17** You may find it easier to achieve your goals now than at other times. **LOWS 2–3; 29–31** Keep a low profile and simply let things be for now.

AUGUST: MAIN TRENDS: 3–4 A time of mental pressure; don't dwell on personal issues if it looks like you can't solve them. Also avoid needless distractions. **10–11** Use this time to plan ahead – no minor detail should escape your notice. Trends suggest your cash flow might improve now. **22–23** As long as you can be out in front and soaking up the limelight, this trend can bring untold social benefits. **KEY DATES: HIGHS 12–14** Use your skills to make progress and build a future in whatever area interests you. **LOWS 26–27** Don't worry if it appears that others are getting ahead of you – it's simply the monthly low patch.

SEPTEMBER: MAIN TRENDS: 1–3 Trends favour communication now, and you may find it easier than usual to talk others around to your way of thinking. **15–16** There may be a need to rein in spending – plan carefully and put something away for a rainy day. **19–20** Your chart reveals that those around you may be inclined to be generous – welcome this with gratitude. **KEY DATES: HIGHS 9–10** You are full of fresh ideas and energy, and the favourable trends for communication continue. **LOWS 22–23** If you feel you can't catch a break; you may need to change your outlook in an ongoing situation.

OCTOBER: MAIN TRENDS: 1–2 You're striking a good balance between self-confidence and empathy – keep this up while you discuss personal issues. **8–9** Your ambition may run counter to the needs of your relationship. Take care to maintain a good balance. **23–24** Personal relationships are your best area now; you may be amazed at the amount of support you now receive. **KEY DATES: HIGHS 6–7** If your intuition says you're making the right moves, that could well mean you are. **LOWS 19–21** A low-key period best spent keeping a low profile.

NOVEMBER: MAIN TRENDS: 6–7 Your affable nature at work makes for a beneficial phase. Note that things go better in pairs just now. **8–9** Sudden events may force you to make a change; be prepared to let go of old notions of security. **21–22** Trends suggest opportunities to meet new people. This is a particularly great time for romantic developments. **KEY DATES: HIGHS 3–4; 30** Expect a sense of achievement as the wheels of progress move properly. **LOWS 15–17** Your endurance will be tested, and all kinds of problems may arise if you can't keep a lid on your ambitions – take time out to rest.

DECEMBER: MAIN TRENDS: 2–3 Enjoy a peaceful home and family life. A good time to redecorate your home or celebrate something. **7–8** If you need to help others then do so, but also make time for solitude. **21–22** You should feel valued both personally and professionally. Nostalgia may be cheering and a situation at work rewarding. **KEY DATES: HIGHS 1; 27–28** A mental peak when your judgment and timing should be unerringly accurate. **LOWS 13–14** Prepare for some hassle during this low patch and remember to look before you leap.

Taurus: your path to success in 2025

TAURUS BORN PEOPLE
Birthdays: 21 April to 21 May inclusive
Planet: Venus. Birthstone: Emerald. Lucky day: Friday

Keynote for the Year: 2025 may find you revising certain friendships and their value to you. Financially, fresh opportunities for monetary gain may be about to come your way.

JANUARY: MAIN TRENDS: 4–5 Set out to broaden your horizons, whether through travel, education, or contact with others. You may gain new insight. **15–16** Trends suggest good results from practical efforts; progress may simply be easier to achieve and help easy to elicit. **20–21** If things have recently been difficult at work, make the most of fresh opportunities – you should be able to improve. **KEY DATES: HIGHS 8–9** This trend may coincide with some personal good luck, but you may also see how you can make your own luck! **LOWS 22–23** Not the best time for making any major move – hang fire for now.

FEBRUARY: MAIN TRENDS: 7–8 Make the most of progressive influences over your career. New information may help you to plan ahead better than ever. **12–13** Current planetary trends indicate that you may need to keep abreast of everything happening around you or recent progress may slide. **20–21** Instinctively, you now have a self-sacrificing quality about you. Recognise that it's impossible to please everyone and don't go to excessive lengths to try. **KEY DATES: HIGHS 4–5** Be open and receptive to new input – something you learn may prove pleasantly lucrative. **LOWS 18–19** Your judgement may be questionable at best, so let partners handle major decisions for now.

MARCH: MAIN TRENDS: 12–13 Your personal life offers the best for you now, so don't feel pressurised by others into prioritising social occasions. **14–15** Some enjoyable times are on the cards as both your social life and love life benefit from some favourable trends. **20–21** New insight and understanding into the strengths and weaknesses of others may enable you to solve some tough problems. **KEY DATES: HIGHS 3–5; 31** Persuasive and charming, you can get others around to your way of thinking. **LOWS 17–19** If your physical energy is lacking, the trick is in knowing when to cease striving – that time is now.

APRIL: MAIN TRENDS: 4–5 Your outlook is now expansive, optimistic and generous, making this a great time for travel, learning, cultural activities and getting more from life. **11–12** A favourable period for getting out and about. You may also find that things go well in a romantic encounter. **21–22** Working with others in groups toward a common goal could benefit you greatly now. You can make quite a difference to someone's life. **KEY DATES: HIGHS 1; 29–30** You could receive unexpected support for a new project if you are prepared to ask. **LOWS 14–15** If a practical matter suffers a setback, look for some damage limitation.

MAY: MAIN TRENDS: 2–3 Friendships and teamwork should be rewarding now. You may find others are willing to do almost anything to help you. **8–10** New ideas prove stimulating, and this may be a good time to assess the progress of certain future aspirations and ambitions. **22–23** Make this an adventurous period – plan a trip or set out to meet new people. **KEY DATES: HIGHS 25–26** In a self-confident mood, your personality shines and these qualities combine to help you succeed in any area. **LOWS 11–12** The low makes you reluctant to compromise which could lead to confrontation. Beware of causing offence.

JUNE: MAIN TRENDS: 10–11 You feel a sense of purpose in pursuing your career goals. You should also be in a good position to influence others' decisions. **15–16** Prepare for some personal changes; it may become obvious that you need to move on in some way, but this will take time. **26–27** Don't put yourself under undue pressure at work – instead accept that you may need to delegate. **KEY DATES: HIGHS 21–22** As the monthly high brings you motivation and drive, a new initiative may pay off.

Taurus: capitalise on your lucky days

LOWS 7–9 If you find yourself at odds with others don't surge ahead blithely ignoring their opinions – they may be right.

JULY: MAIN TRENDS: 1–2 Don't be afraid to pursue independent interests. You enjoy dealing with new ideas and can explain them to others effectively. **10–11** Work life may be challenging now, but you can still make beginnings and bold moves; just make sure they're worth fighting for. **21–22** Home will be your favourite place now as positive planetary trends ruling the domestic scene do you the world of good and provide a real sense of security. **KEY DATES: HIGHS 18–19** Things at work improve, and with superiors on your side you may be able to reach your goals. **LOWS 4–6** The monthly low hampers your ambitions – better to watch and wait for now.

AUGUST: MAIN TRENDS: 4–6 Relationships with colleagues function nicely as you delegate and successfully enlist others' co-operation when required. **8–9** Success and progress at work is a real possibility right now – the more ambitious you are, the better. **23–25** Trends move on and now, facing obstacles in your path, ambition may seem more trouble than it's worth. Try not to let this feeling overwhelm you. **KEY DATES: HIGHS 15–16** Use a little ingenuity to improve your efficiency and help you get ahead. **LOWS 28–30** The low patch finds you preferring your own company, so avoid work or social commitments if you can.

SEPTEMBER: MAIN TRENDS: 5–6 A quiet period socially is forecast, although there's much to keep you happy and fulfilled with your personal schedule. **15–16** Travel and intellectual interests are positively highlighted and you value the freedom to roam and enjoy the outdoors. **22–23** An improvement to all matters professional: don't be afraid to use your initiative as you plan some significant changes. **KEY DATES: HIGHS 11–12** Productive and with energy to spare, you can now complete things in half the usual time. **LOWS 24–26** Some matters at home may need to be addressed but – beware – unrealistic thinking may result in confusion.

OCTOBER: MAIN TRENDS: 1–2 A favourable time to discuss a new idea with someone, especially in business. A visit to somewhere new may provide inspiration for fresh interests. **12–13** You are kind and empathetic, but make sure this isn't misplaced – beware of someone leading you up the garden path! **24–25** Trends make you rather an expert in social relationships now, skilled in initiating meetings and smoothing over any difficulties. **KEY DATES: HIGHS 8–9** Personal and business encounters work out favourably; even minor conflicts may reap a creative reward. **LOWS 22–23** A pressurised phase – avoid confrontation over responsibilities and let partners handle major decisions.

NOVEMBER: MAIN TRENDS: 3–4 Trends place a positive influence over work and property. Expect some good, productive developments. Also, a good time to build upon recent efforts to get ahead in any area. **11–13** Popular with friends and colleagues alike you attract a lot of goodwill that could be an invaluable asset at work. **21–22** Enjoy the closeness and emotional support of your partner and confide in those who mean the most to you. **KEY DATES: HIGHS 5–6** It's a good time to begin something new as work goes smoothly and your ideas are ingenious. **LOWS 18–19** Beware a tendency to be over-emotional. Avoid accidents that could arise from a lack of concentration.

DECEMBER: MAIN TRENDS: 5–6 Don't rely on the bright lights of your social life to cheer you up, instead focus on always being yourself, especially if you must contend with the egos of others. **17–18** Clear communication is called for if it appears that others aren't listening to you. Consider taking time out for some independent pursuits. **20–21** This trend is all about broadening mental horizons – seek out others on a similar wavelength and focus on the cultural side of life. **KEY DATES: HIGHS 2–3; 29–31** Lady Luck is with you, so go for what you really want and a little good fortune may follow. **LOWS 15–17** It would be wise to delay the start of a plan of action until this low point is over.

Gemini: how to get ahead in 2025

GEMINI BORN PEOPLE
Birthdays: 22 May to 21 June inclusive
Planet: Mercury. Birthstone: Agate. Lucky day: Wednesday

Keynote for the Year: *Lucky Jupiter occupies your sign until mid-June so use these months to strike while the iron's hot and keep a look-out for opportunities to advance.*

JANUARY: MAIN TRENDS: 3–5 Don't be over concerned if not all your endeavours pay dividends. Even fifty per cent success should now be good enough. **7–8** Everyday life keeps you on the go, as it should – but keep your eyes and ears open for news relating to a special project. **20–21** Confide in your partner or spouse and you could find their response both beneficial and emotionally rewarding. **KEY DATES: HIGHS 10–11** Trends suggest that plans should go your way and the more ambitious you are, the better. **LOWS 24–26** The monthly low brings some emotional challenges, especially if you still need to get something off your chest.

FEBRUARY: MAIN TRENDS: 8–10 Professional obligations could now detract from your personal life but ultimately something may force you to get your act together. **16–17** Expect to be in tune with both yourself and companions and perhaps to make some new friends. **19–20** Your chart reveals the possibility of a major leap forward. Don't be afraid to entertain new ideas, you may find they fit into your life in an unexpected way. **KEY DATES: HIGHS 6–7** Make the most of the here and now and you should find yourself speeding towards your goals. **LOWS 22–23** Beware a tendency to overextend yourself; do what you can then get an early night.

MARCH: MAIN TRENDS: 4–6 You're focused on the future, especially in your career, and current trends may assist your desire for personal advancement. **15–16** Follow your heart if something needs to change, or you need fresh mental stimulation; a less structured attitude to life may help. **22–23** A rewarding time domestically, possibly involving exciting family news or good times with friends. **KEY DATES: HIGHS 6–7** A quick decision may turn out better than expected if you take the initiative. **LOWS 20–21** Approach all matters methodically and beware of potential pitfalls.

APRIL: MAIN TRENDS: 6–7 Use your energy for practical tasks now – working under pressure will bring out the best in you. **15–17** Trends place a positive influence over your love life now. Enjoy quality time with your partner and perhaps plan a wonderful surprise. **21–22** Your intuition and analytical insight is sharply honed, enabling you to get to the heart of things. Make sure you consult a partner before you take any action though. **KEY DATES: HIGHS 2–3; 29–30** A cautious gamble may pay off at this generally positive time. **LOWS 16–18** Pace yourself while you fulfil your obligations as you're lacking energy now.

MAY: MAIN TRENDS: 9–10 Avoid unnecessary confrontation, be consistent and keep yourself busy. **17–19** Family life should be most fulfilling now; relive the past in some way and stay close to what you find comforting. **21–22** Someone may take you into their confidence and need help getting to the core of a problem to find a successful solution. Expect to feel rightly proud of your achievement. **KEY DATES: HIGHS 27–28** Big things are afoot in your chart – just about anything can happen if you make it. **LOWS 13–15** Making plans during the lunar low is never a good idea; hang fire and ride out this trend.

JUNE: MAIN TRENDS: 3–4 Getting out and about may now lead into unfamiliar territory – this is a good thing, so enjoy what you encounter on your travels. **5–6** Your enthusiasm could be contagious, and you make wonderful, upbeat company. **21–22** A fulfilling phase for your emotional and family life. In a sensitive and caring frame of mind, others are ready to reciprocate and offer you the support you

Gemini: what do the stars hold for you?

need. **KEY DATES: HIGHS 23–24** With swift action comes achievement under this trend, so back your hunches now. **LOWS 10–11** Avoid entering into any contracts or making long-term commitments until the lunar low has properly passed. You may lack the confidence to do so, anyway.

JULY: MAIN TRENDS: 8–9 You may be set a challenge that ultimately leads you to broaden your point of view; you may come to see that you don't know it all, after all! **16–17** Boundless energy combined with initiative will help you complete a fun project in a timely manner. **24–25** Your self-assurance gives you a magnetic quality that attracts others; you, in turn, will enjoy being centre-stage and put your charms to good use. **KEY DATES: HIGHS 20–22** A long-term plan looks set to come to a triumphant conclusion. **LOWS 7–8** You may feel powerless, but it will help if you are ready to change with circumstances as they happen.

AUGUST: MAIN TRENDS: 7–8 Focus on your career now – there may be an opportunity to get ahead in your chosen profession and put the finishing touches to a project. **22–23** Current trends make you vulnerable to deception. Be cautious about most things, but especially about unsolicited advice. **28–29** Prepare for a change that will force you to adapt or to abandon something you judge to be past its sell-by-date. **KEY DATES: HIGHS 17–18** Put your persuasive talents to good use in the workplace. **LOWS 3–4; 31** A break from the norm may do you the world of good – a real break that is, from *everything*!

SEPTEMBER: MAIN TRENDS: 3–5 Trends suggest you may be exposed to new ideas and philosophies that can nicely broaden your outlook on life. Long distance travel could also prove richly rewarding. **10–11** The planetary focus is now on work making this a great time to consolidate your recent efforts and build up your resources. **22–23** As the pace of events speeds up you will be ploughing your own furrow at work, and you won't let anything stand in your way. **KEY DATES: HIGHS 13–14** A favourable time for Gemini, especially if you have a choice to make – the right path should be clear to you. **LOWS 1; 27–28** Do what you must to keep the wheels of progress turning, then get some rest.

OCTOBER: MAIN TRENDS: 1–2 Take stock of your current situation; you may need to be rid of some non-essential elements. Begin by asking yourself if anything is holding you back. **5–6** This is a very auspicious influence for all professional matters. Use your diplomatic skills in a work situation to improve your position. **27–28** Your engaging style may make you popular now, but you will benefit from activities requiring quick thinking or direct action. **KEY DATES: HIGHS 10–11** The signposts to success should be obvious – just follow them. **LOWS 24–26** Tread carefully if you encounter an obstacle or delay making a move until after the low has passed.

NOVEMBER: MAIN TRENDS: 2–3 Another favourable time to broaden your horizons and get into something new. Push yourself beyond your everyday world. **12–13** At work, you might have to make a snap major decision if your objective is to be attained – but remember that decisive does not mean rash. **23–24** Trends now favour your personal relationships. You are entertaining company, but you will want to be the centre of attention. **KEY DATES: HIGHS 7–8** New ideas can foster new opportunities – a time for innovation and invention. **LOWS 20–22** Weigh up your options carefully and assess the whole picture before you set any goals.

DECEMBER: MAIN TRENDS: 6–7 Look out for an opportunity to get ahead at work; if you say the right things to the right people, events could go your way. **9–10** Focus on spending time with friends, although you should enjoy anything involving group or team effort. **21–22** Financial issues may become easier to negotiate, and perhaps you can afford to be generous, you may simply feel more in control of economic matters. **KEY DATES: HIGHS 4–5** Seize the chance to start a new project if it is offered to you. **LOWS 18–19** The lunar low saps your energy levels – be patient and ride out the trend.

Please name FOULSHAM'S ALMANACK when replying to advertisers

Old Moore now Introduces you to Master Kuang and the Whispering Wisdom of your
CHINESE HOROSCOPE
EVERY DAY – IF YOU LIKE

Let Old Moore introduce you to his friend **Kuang C. Wang**. He is the great Chinese Master, whom Old Moore has invited to join his *personalised daily advice service*. By allowing Master Kuang the use of his new and massive computer, Old Moore can provide you with new, top quality Chinese guidance and wisdom thinking.

There is here a motivational thought for you every day.

Your daily rendezvous with Old Moore's friend, Kuang C. Wang will cost but a few pence per day* and you can hear this authoritative guide to your life, work and happiness. This is not the usual 'fortune telling' patter, but enlightened insights into how best to exploit your potential on any given day.

Unlike any other astro phone service, Master Kuang will be working from the day, month and year of your birth to give you the most individual predictions at the lift of a phone. Ring this number and discover the most truly personalised advice.

Down the centuries, successful Chinese people have used the benefits of their ancient wisdom systems. In their daily living, they draw upon a cocktail of positive guidance. They use Astrology, Feng Shui, I-Ching and carefully selected *whispering thoughts of wisdom* to guide them for each coming day.

Yes, every day, the Chinese system combines its elements to produce thoughts of *wisdom*, which can help you to get the best out of any day.

Today there is such a thought for you. Your Guiding Principle for the day. And you can carry it through the day to help your intuitive powers. They can so greatly improve your life. And the decisions you make during the day.

0906 880 5493

*Calls cost 60p per minute at all times
Charges may be higher for payphones and non-BT networks
Complaints & Service Provider (ATS): 0844 836 9769

2025 – The Year of the Snake

Chinese astrology works on a slightly different time scale from the more familiar Western branch of the study, and because of this Chinese New Year is marked on a different date each year. It is not, therefore, until 29 January in 2025 that the new year is celebrated, and the Year of the Snake officially begins. At the beginning of 2025, the world is still under the rulership of the outgoing and positive Dragon, and so a high action period with plenty of activity can be expected.

Snake years are times when the world stops to think. Unlike the progressive Dragon, the Snake epitomises patience, although we all know that snakes can be dangerous when they decide to strike. While there should be fewer arguments on the international scene, governments may be using this time to build up resources for their arsenals. The Western zodiac sign associated with the Snake is Taurus the Bull, an ever-patient animal but one that has great strength and power when he chooses to use it.

The Element associated with the Snake during 2025 is Wood. This suits the considered nature of the Snake, ensuring a year of some comfort, and a slow and steady rise in global economic fortunes. Under the influence of Wood, world leaders may prove to be quite reasonable, whilst across the planet this is likely to be a time when people's tastes change quite dramatically and fashions and styles from the past will once again return.

We should see a more settled year than the previous one under the influence of the fiery Dragon. Issues are resolved, mostly to universal satisfaction, and international trade should be improving. This is a particularly good year for China, so we can expect that country to be moving ahead at a pace, whilst outright revolutions of the sort that were common a year or two ago are much less likely with the Snake in charge. There should be less fluctuation on international stock markets and a degree of stability seems to reign.

If you were born under the sign of the Snake, which generally speaking would mean your birthday fell in 1917, 1929, 1941, 1953, 1965, 1977, 1989, 2001 or 2013 you can expect 2025 to work very well for you. You will be firing on all cylinders, anxious to get moving and you will not easily be diverted from your plans. Caution is always your watchword, but you should be able to bring ideas to fruition.

Snakes are generally calculating and have staggering patience. You have a good, if somewhat odd, sense of humour and you tend to make friends that you keep for a very long time. You approach life differently to others because you are less interested in immediate gratification. In relationships you are kind, sympathetic and empathetic, but occasionally a little distant and not the most outgoing person in the world. You may find it slightly difficult to express your emotions. Snakes are often artistic and like to live in a comfortable and clean environment. You are as much a watcher of life as a participator. You adore summer warmth and tend to withdraw in cold weather, just as your Chinese sign would.

Cancer: your planetary highlights in 2025

CANCER BORN PEOPLE
Birthdays: 22 June to 22 July inclusive
Planet: Moon. Birthstone: Ruby. Lucky day: Monday

Keynote for the Year: *If you can remain flexible in your ideas the sky's the limit from July, as opportunistic Jupiter helps you grow in every area of life.*

JANUARY: MAIN TRENDS: 2–3 As the year begins, you feel secure in your career with positive things happening at work. **15–16** Trends bring you the ability to win others over as you thrive on teamwork and any group activities. **20–21** Travel and communications are highlighted in your chart now. A new way of thinking could be the answer to your problems. **KEY DATES: HIGHS 12–13** You may find you are in a strong position to determine the course of events at work – make the most of it. **LOWS 27–28** Keep things simple and go with the flow during the monthly lunar low.

FEBRUARY: MAIN TRENDS: 5–6 You are energetic and may seem quite assertive. Beware – you've little patience for people who seem to be in your way. **17–18** A go-ahead phase is underway, and your pursuit of power and status seems unstoppable – let nothing stand in its way, then! **19–20** Latch on to the chance to learn something new. Your determination to achieve your ambitions is also key now. **KEY DATES: HIGHS 8–10** Optimism and positive thinking will make an ever-greater difference to your life. **LOWS 23–24** You may feel constrained and personal glory will be hard to come by. Opt for a low-key approach.

MARCH: MAIN TRENDS: 11–12 Take advice from someone in a position of influence before you consider an important change. **14–15** Trends suggest that things go better in pairs right now, especially in practical or business matters. **20–21** Events in every arena of life may put you to the test, but there is no need for this to become a problem – you thrive on challenge and will win in the end. **KEY DATES: HIGHS 8–9** In the mood for exploration and expansion, this is the perfect time to plan ahead. **LOWS 22–24** This monthly low patch points to a time when various 'red lights' could be holding you back. Proceed with caution.

APRIL: MAIN TRENDS: 6–7 Finding good company will be no trouble for you now – this is an excellent time for forming new social contacts, and you seem to be just about everyone's favourite person. **8–9** Don't be afraid to be assertive and move forward in whatever way you like; you have all the drive and energy you could want, and it should be easy to channel it. **21–22** If you feel under pressure, take decisive action. You may find you are able to bring certain projects to a successful conclusion. **KEY DATES: HIGHS 4–5** The monthly high makes you quick off the mark, especially at work. **LOWS 19–20** Be prepared for progress to only come in fits and starts and don't let this worry you.

MAY: MAIN TRENDS: 5–6 Trends reveal that this is a time for 'off with the old, on with the new'. Take whatever steps you can here, but don't rush any decisions. **13–14** Although you are in a super-confident mood, take care not to come on too strong with others. While fun is high on your agenda, others may not share your enthusiasm. **21–22** Travel is indicated in your chart, and this will eliminate any boredom. If you get a chance to get out and about, take it. **KEY DATES: HIGHS 1; 29–30** Start a new project or begin a new venture – under these trends, the potential for growth is great. **LOWS 16–17** Be alert for a potentially deceptive influence in communications. Ask friends or family for advice if you suspect a scam.

JUNE: MAIN TRENDS: 4–6 Trends suggest that the need to transform your life may now reach a turning point, and much will depend upon the actions you take now. The way ahead looks positive. **16–17** Take care to think before you speak as some of your views may be contentious. **21–22** Trends

Cancer: tune into your favourable days

bring family relationships into prominence, which could mean an enjoyably nostalgic time reliving memories from the past or, perhaps, meetings with old faces. **KEY DATES: HIGHS 25–26** Aim for your objectives, whether personal or professional. **LOWS 12–13** Be sure not to promise more than you can realistically deliver.

JULY: MAIN TRENDS: 4–5 Trends suggest you could make some important contacts through work, while colleagues and bosses should be generally helpful. **7–8** Others may come across as rather assertive so try to strike a balance between standing your ground and being understanding. **21–22** Your willingness to battle against the odds may stand you in good stead at work. **KEY DATES: HIGHS 23–24** Use your considerable energy for new initiatives. Some quick thinking may help you out of a tricky spot. **LOWS 9–11** Pay close attention to detail and small print during this time.

AUGUST: MAIN TRENDS: 1–2 A long-term project may come to a successful conclusion. Decisions made now may powerfully affect the future. **15–17** Prepare for a high-spirited time when easy charm should come as second nature and you will enjoy being the centre of attention. **22–23** The planets now benefit all your relationships and give you much to keep you inspired. Talks and meetings tend to go in your favour. **KEY DATES: HIGHS 19–20** This month's lunar high could bring you something of the Midas touch. Think big, for a change. **LOWS 6–7** Don't give in to half-baked, misdirected plans – if you need a rethink, take the time.

SEPTEMBER: MAIN TRENDS: 4–5 Your chart suggests that you may be feeling unusually sensitive but don't let this spoil social affairs. A past matter may preoccupy but be aware that its relevance is only to you. **10–11** Trends now favour domestic matters; take some time to resolve issues as well as to enjoy entertainment and social activities in the home. **22–23** Your personal life may come under scrutiny; be as open as possible about your feelings with those close to you. **KEY DATES: HIGHS 15–16** Lady Luck might now help you with anything on your wish list. **LOWS 2–3; 29–30** Take a step back and rest for a while.

OCTOBER: MAIN TRENDS: 7–8 Take a look at your finances to see if you can capitalise on any recent events. Planetary changes indicate that this is a good time to turn ideas into profitable reality – but take professional advice before you make any significant move. **15–16** Make an early start at work as trends continue to favour the monetary sphere. **23–24** Energetic, strong and confident, it's time to put your creative gifts to use or make the most of a current romance. **KEY DATES: HIGHS 12–13** Success may come via an unexpected route. **LOWS 27–28** Don't jump to conclusions about others and try not to be oversensitive.

NOVEMBER: MAIN TRENDS: 2–3 Trends suggest a new breakthrough in your career that could lead to good prospects in the long term. **5–6** You're intuitive and co-operative, use these heightened skills to get a joint plan off the ground. **22–23** A practical matter may leave you feeling insecure; take time out to spend in solitude and find out what's really driving you. **KEY DATES: HIGHS 9–10** The planets indicate a lucky result from a measured gamble – but make sure to think things through before you act. Never gamble money you cannot afford to lose. **LOWS 23–24** Rein things in and take a step back during the low patch.

DECEMBER: MAIN TRENDS: 9–10 A problem can only hold you back if you let it. Be positive and all will be well. **14–16** Throw off outworn situations and use your shrewd intuition to good effect. **21–22** The outdoor life holds the most interest for you now, and a pre-Christmas mini break is especially favoured. **KEY DATES: HIGHS 6–7** This month's lunar high brings you closer than ever to realising your dreams. **LOWS 20–22** Make sure to keep control over minor issues but also be aware of your own limitations.

Leo: how to make the most of 2025

LEO BORN PEOPLE
Birthdays: 23 July to 23 August inclusive
Planet: Sun. Birthstone: Sapphire. Lucky day: Sunday

Keynote for the Year: *Addressing issues of the past may bring healing this year, as you seek to settle certain financial matters once and for all.*

JANUARY: MAIN TRENDS: 7–9 You may realise that long-held ambitions are longer relevant to you or hold the same attraction – plan ahead for a clean break if necessary. **12–13** Events behind closed doors are reassuring and domestic relationships particularly rewarding now. **20–21** Your chart reveals this as the crucial period for renewal and regeneration. Get down to business and strip away unwanted things from the past. **KEY DATES: HIGHS 14–16** You are intuitively tuned to changes in 'atmosphere' – follow your instincts wherever they lead. **LOWS 29–30** Postpone any unnecessary plans during the lunar low, especially at work.

FEBRUARY: MAIN TRENDS: 8–9 In a restless mood now, the last thing you want to be doing is mundane tasks. Look for what you enjoy but be sure to keep material affairs ticking over. **13–14** Expect some competition in social events now but be aware that co-operation with others will lead to the best outcomes. **19–20** Your cheery mood may prove infectious, as may your sense of romance. Should be a lot of fun! **KEY DATES: HIGHS 11–12** If you're ready to accept changes for the better, this can be a time of expansion and ambition. **LOWS 25–26** Be realistic and know your limitations, especially in the workplace.

MARCH: MAIN TRENDS: 1–2 You're at your best in social and romantic situations – use your creative self-expression to good effect. **8–9** Put your quick mind to work in practical matters and you may come up with some ingenious ideas. New input from a co-worker may prove valuable. **20–21** Whatever you handle now you may want to get at its deepest roots. You could learn something of significant value through a personal relationship. **KEY DATES: HIGHS 10–11** In a dynamic frame of mind, this is an excellent time to plan for the future. **LOWS 25–26** Trends suggest you should prepare for a short, but temporary, setback.

APRIL: MAIN TRENDS: 1–3 Trends suggest some success at work; you may receive some unexpected human assistance as well as planetary! **9–10** A lift for friendships as you should be taking life in your stride and be enjoyable company for others. **23–24** Beware of unwarranted optimism right now – this is not the time to gamble or to take chances. Don't promise more than you can deliver. **KEY DATES: HIGHS 6–8** Under this influence you are inspired to tackle any problem. Success may follow. **LOWS 21–22** Be alert for pitfalls in any area of life; things can go awry even when you are not the one at fault.

MAY: MAIN TRENDS: 7–8 The planets put you in a changeable mood and make it hard for you to see things objectively. Time spent in contemplation may help you develop a clearer sense of self. **15–16** Socially a very beneficial time when your excellent motivational skills help broaden your horizons immeasurably. **22–23** Now you can afford to be magnanimous, as you recognise the good in others. Most aspects of daily life fall nicely into place, but especially at work. **KEY DATES: HIGHS 3–4** Stimulating new ideas and opportunities may be on offer and this is the perfect time to act. **LOWS 18–19** The lunar low is never the right time to make important changes – wait until this phase has passed.

JUNE: MAIN TRENDS: 4–6 You know what to do to make a good impression on others, but your real strength lies in enlisting their help and assistance. **11–12** Professional matters (even with challenges) seem to work out; trust your instincts on the likely outcome of certain plans. **21–22** In one-to-one

Leo: plan into your favourable days

relationships you should be bringing out the best in each other – take this opportunity to express your affection. **KEY DATES: HIGHS 1; 27–28** With boundless energy and the luck of the planets behind you, put a long-held plan into action. **LOWS 14–16** Prepare for a little disorganisation in your private life and simply roll with the changes.

JULY: MAIN TRENDS: 1–2 With confidence and natural ebullience, you make rather entertaining company for others. **3–4** Look ahead with continued faith in yourself and your abilities. Your best advantages are likely to be in a professional environment. **22–23** Good organisation at work is the key to avoiding setbacks, but even with this your progress may not be as marked as you'd like for a couple of days. **KEY DATES: HIGHS 25–26** Trends move on, and this is now a positive period when every step you take seems to be in the right direction. **LOWS 12–13** Avoid the obstacles of the low patch and save your energy for better periods.

AUGUST: MAIN TRENDS: 4–5 Multi-tasking will be your speciality now; put your ingenuity and versatility to some good use in any area of life that appeals to you. **18–19** Teamwork and group events have lots to offer in the way of fulfilment, especially if they involve friends. **23–24** You make impressive company now and could have an uplifting effect on others, but don't let your ego run out of control. **KEY DATES: HIGHS 21–22** Enjoy the company of others and the positive effect it has on you. **LOWS 8–9** If there are tasks that must be performed, process them methodically and don't bite off more than you can chew.

SEPTEMBER: MAIN TRENDS: 7–8 With Venus in your sign, your love life is full of potential. A great time to seek new friendships, or maybe attract them. **12–13** Life can be ever so inspiring if you get out and about and soak up a little culture. Personally, you may be winding a project up. **23–24** Your powers of attraction remain in the ascendant, and this continues to be a great time for love and social life. **KEY DATES: HIGHS 17–19** A little measured risk could help a plan of action but think carefully before you make a move. **LOWS 4–6** Caution will be needed if you must make a decision – delay it if you can.

OCTOBER: MAIN TRENDS: 6–7 Use your time constructively now to devise new plans or make meaningful progress with recent ones, particularly around finance. **8–9** A helpful trend for practical matters; you may benefit from a little advance information concerning your next task. **24–25** Don't expect things to be perfectly organised at work – even the best laid plans could go awry, so leave room for errors. **KEY DATES: HIGHS 14–16** Not a time to stand still – get out and about to make valuable new contacts. **LOWS 2–3; 29–30** Absorbed by career commitments now, prepare to encounter some professional obstacles that call for tough decisions.

NOVEMBER: MAIN TRENDS: 3–4 An excellent time for pleasurable pursuits and socialising – time to plan a party, or an outing of some kind. **7–8** Refuse to take on any new tasks or start anything afresh until previous issues are cleared up for good. You would be wise to keep life simple. **22–23** One of your better times to enjoy a little personal freedom, whether through travel or interaction with others. A change of environment may be all that you need. **KEY DATES: HIGHS 11–12** A productive phase when professional progress should be easy to achieve. **LOWS 25–27** You may lose confidence in certain goals – avoid making long-term commitments but defend your interests.

DECEMBER: MAIN TRENDS: 1–3 There's much to be said for relying on others and taking a back seat in decision-making under the current trends. **14–15** Although superficially energetic and commanding, underneath this façade you should play your cards close to your chest, especially in financial matters. **21–22** Try to push ahead with a work objective before the Christmas break; it may lead to an opportunity for leadership. **KEY DATES: HIGHS 8–9** Relish the rare chance to let some projects simply run their natural course. **LOWS 23–24** A winding down kind of influence – enjoy a period of quiet reflection and contemplation.

Virgo: your daily guide to 2025

VIRGO BORN PEOPLE
Birthdays: 24 August to 23 September inclusive
Planet: Mercury. Birthstone: Sardonyx. Lucky day: Wednesday

Keynote for the Year: *You may feel that it's all or nothing in your relationship this year as you strive to resolve some personal issues. Expect a good start to the year professionally.*

JANUARY: MAIN TRENDS: 2–3 Begin the year by throwing off your personal boundaries and seeking freedom through travel if you can. This is also an excellent time for intellectual or cultural interests and discussions. **9–11** Demonstrate your leadership skills as your competitive drive, initiative and energy are boosted. **20–21** Your efforts should reap rewards if you are ambitious and don't let self-doubt hold you back. **KEY DATES: HIGHS 17–18** You are optimistic, enthusiastic and self-confident – go for it! **LOWS 4–5; 31** Watch your own motives carefully during this time and learn from any mistakes.

FEBRUARY: MAIN TRENDS: 7–9 The pace of life should be extremely busy over these three days; prepare for lots of contact with others and, perhaps, some good news to lift your spirits. **10–11** Stick around familiar faces and places. The past looms large right now and is a reassuring presence. **19–20** As the strength of your personality has an impact on others, trends suggest that a new friendship may be on the horizon. **KEY DATES: HIGHS 13–14** You seem to hold the secret to popularity now, so put it to good use. **LOWS 1; 27–28** You may feel the need for change and growth but take care not to uproot your own security.

MARCH: MAIN TRENDS: 5–6 This influence may hamper your motivation to get things done, but it also brings domestic fulfilment and enjoyment of hearth and home. **17–18** A productive period so put yourself in the thick of things; meetings and appointments should go swimmingly. **20–21** Change things up if you can or, even better, go in search of new intellectual experiences. Travel is positively highlighted for Virgoans, now. **KEY DATES: HIGHS 12–14** Events occur that help you to overcome most (if not all) problems and get ahead. **LOWS 27–28** A personal matter may be too difficult to resolve now, and patience is the only solution.

APRIL: MAIN TRENDS: 1–2 This influence may bring zest for life and energy to channel into brand new projects – for sheer pace no one can beat you now. **4–5** Maintain a high a profile, especially at work. You may receive some news regarding a professional matter that you can later put to good use. **21–22** If a recent project isn't working accept that you may have to abandon it, no matter how much you may want to hang on to it. **KEY DATES: HIGHS 9–10** In an ambitious mood, you may feel the sky's the limit. Make the most of this feeling. **LOWS 23–24** Take things easily and keep your objectives within easy reach.

MAY: MAIN TRENDS: 3–4 This may not be the best time for getting your own way with your partner. Avoid acting in ways that might cause others – especially loved ones – to work against you. **13–14** You're the centre of attention as you enjoy the social limelight – show off your talents a little and relish the starring role! **23–25** An emotional matter may prove tense and patience is in short supply – the taking-the-bull-by-the-horns approach won't work; grace under pressure may. **KEY DATES: HIGHS 6–7** Assume a leading role and persuade others around to your side in any debate as your judgement should prove spot on. **LOWS 21–22** Put your plans on the back burner and lend a hand to someone in need.

JUNE: MAIN TRENDS: 4–5 The desire to break out of your shell will help you attract new friends. Relationships should be rewarding, and you won't want for company for too long. **6–7** Resolve a previously pressing problem by looking for an original solution. You can discard a pressing problem or situation. **21–22** Trends point to material security through partnerships; there may be new money-

Virgo: get in touch with your planetary rhythms

making opportunities in joint financial and business ventures. **KEY DATES: HIGHS 2–3** You have plans to change things and the necessary power to do so. Now is the time. **LOWS 17–18** Something might be testing your patience – accept that you can't expect too much in the way of progress during the monthly low.

JULY: MAIN TRENDS: 9–10 Use your Virgoan flair for detail and take on a role as organiser, whether with information or with people. **11–12** Important news may require swift action and some fast thinking; once you have done so, you may reap the benefits. **22–23** A nice spell at home and a relaxing and rewarding time for all domestic matters, especially if you were considering any creative or DIY improvements. **KEY DATES: HIGHS 1; 27–28** Your competitive spirits revive – get ready to make whatever changes are needed, especially at work. **LOWS 14–15** A slightly listless period; roll with the punches and delay important decisions.

AUGUST: MAIN TRENDS: 1–2 You may receive some interesting information but be sure to check it carefully before taking any decisive action based upon it. **15–16** Let go and express yourself – although you may not find the audience you wanted, it's still a good time to dominate the spotlight. **26–27** Set out to broaden your social horizons; there ought to be plenty of inspiration out there among friends and acquaintances. **KEY DATES: HIGHS 23–25** Put your capacity for ruthless efficiency to good use. **LOWS 10–11** Be prepared to make some serious compromises to get what you want.

SEPTEMBER: MAIN TRENDS: 3–4 You could afford to be more ambitious at work, though it seems you simply want to see a job done well and are prepared to work hard. **12–13** A lively atmosphere permeates all your relationships, and you should be able to get along wonderfully with just about anyone. **23–24** Not quite the kind of atmosphere you'd like at work – you may find a professional partner with a bee in their bonnet over something you find unimportant. **KEY DATES: HIGHS 20–21** Seize any opportunity to get out in front during the lunar high. **LOWS 7–8** Try to avoid a demanding situation – there are potential pitfalls ahead.

OCTOBER: MAIN TRENDS: 9–10 A steady time for progress at work; aim to take charge and make meaningful changes that impact on the longer term. **11–12** Your love life ought to be on a roll and you may come to realise how easy it is to get along with your partner. **23–24** Despite a sense of vigour and determination, your power to influence life in any remarkable way may be limited now. But support may arise through partnerships. **KEY DATES: HIGHS 17–18** Be energetic and competitive and make full use of your increased vitality and self-confidence. **LOWS 4–5** Forget something that's not really working and chalk it up to experience.

NOVEMBER: MAIN TRENDS: 5–6 Practical tasks offer your best moments. Note that there may be more than one way of getting ahead at work. **17–18** You may feel quite optimistic over a new project but bear in mind that while it may look financially lucrative, it may be early days. **22–23** While there may be interesting ideas in the air, there may not be time to do everything you'd planned, so don't scatter your energies. **KEY DATES: HIGHS 13–14** Spirits and motivation run high, so set out to accomplish all you can. **LOWS 1–2; 28–29** This is not your most productive time so set aside heavy tasks, if possible.

DECEMBER: MAIN TRENDS: 2–3 Social invitations come thick and fast, and you are in the mood for some fun. **17–18** Unrealistic thinking may lead to mistakes – a little more of your usual common sense is all that's needed. **22–23** Go forth and show the world just how bright you are – social encounters now may prove the source of much useful information. **KEY DATES: HIGHS 10–12** A very good time to do those things which you previously put off. **LOWS 25–26** A contemplative Christmas when you may ponder your recent decisions.

Please name FOULSHAM'S ALMANACK when replying to advertisers

The UK's Leading Psychic Service
Voted No.1 by Customers

Visit Us Online :: www.Trusted-Psychics.co.uk

One of the highest respected psychic services bringing hope and comfort to thousands of callers across the world. Our handpicked readers are passionate about their work, to offer you future clarity, whatever your circumstances.

What We Can Offer You
★ Love Questions Answered In Clear Expert Detail
★ Work / Career / Money / Finance Readings
★ Unique Horoscope / Astrology Predictions
★ Family / Friends Detailed Readings Online
★ Mediumship / Personal Spirit Messages
★ Clairvoyant Specialist Readings Online
★ Personal Clear Future Life Predictions
★ Incredible Handpicked Tarot Readers

NO.1 PSYCHIC TEAM

Start Your Personal Reading Today

 Call Us Today 0906 360 7385

 Credit Card VISA MasterCard **0121 620 2222**

 Text Your Questions 07458 122 322

Cheapest Psychic Readings

Call our dedicated team of experienced Psychics, Mediums, Clairvoyants, Fortune Tellers and Tarot readers commited in offering clear guidance about your life's future path. **Excellence is our only standard.**

★★★★★ Love & Relationship Experts

Love Specialists

Clairvoyants

Mediumship

Service by LiveLines UK Ltd. Calls cost 65p plus network access charges apply. We send promo msgs, call Helpline 03332002321 to opt out. Calls recorded. 18+ only. PO6538 NN2 7YN. Payments@livelinesuk.com.

JANUARY

For High Water add 5h 30m for Bristol, 4h 23m for Hull, 0h 43m for Leith; subtract 2h 21m for Dublin, 1h 26m for Greenock, 2h 29m for Liverpool.

D of M	D of W	Festivals, Events and Anniversaries	Sun at London Rises	Sun at London Sets	High Water at London Bridge am	High Water at London Bridge pm	Moon at London Rises	Moon at London Sets	Weather
			h m	h m	h m	h m	h m	h m	
1	W	New Year's Day	08:06	16:02	02:25	14:48	09:47	17:29	Beginning with a pattern of expected winter weather conditions, this is followed by significant breaks with less wind. Some storms occurring at the start, especially in the north.
2	Th	Bank holiday (Scotland)	08:05	16:03	03:05	15:30	10:11	18:55	
3	F	Derek Draper d. 2024	08:05	16:04	03:44	16:12	10:28	20:22	
4	Sa	World Braille Day	08:05	16:05	04:23	16:55	10:42	21:46	
5	Su	Battle of Nancy 1477	08:05	16:07	05:02	17:40	10:55	23:10	
6	M	Epiphany	08:04	16:08	05:44	18:29	11:07	—	
7	Tu	Krays arrested 1965	08:04	16:09	06:30	19:25	11:20	00:35	
8	W	1st State of Union 1790	08:03	16:10	07:27	20:30	11:35	02:01	
9	Th	Princess of Wales b. 1982	08:03	16:12	08:44	21:38	11:56	03:30	
10	F	Texas strikes oil 1901	08:02	16:13	10:02	22:48	12:25	04:59	
11	Sa	Annie Nightingale d. 2024	08:02	16:15	11:15	23:57	13:07	06:22	
12	Su	Des O'Connor b. 1932	08:01	16:16	—	—	14:07	07:30	
13	M	World University Games op	08:00	16:18	00:56	13:18	15:21	08:20	
14	Tu	Sidereal winter solstice	08:00	16:19	01:45	14:08	16:43	08:54	
15	W	British Museum op. 1759	07:59	16:21	02:29	14:53	18:05	09:17	
16	Th	Prohibition in force 1920	07:58	16:22	03:09	15:35	19:23	09:34	
17	F	Michelle Obama b. 1964	07:57	16:24	03:46	16:13	20:38	09:46	
18	Sa	Sir Cecil Beaton d. 1980	07:56	16:25	04:20	16:49	21:50	09:57	
19	Su	Louis XVI executed 1793	07:55	16:27	04:52	17:22	23:00	10:06	
20	M	Duchess/Edinburgh b. 1905	07:54	16:29	05:23	17:55	—	10:16	
21	Tu	George Orwell d. 1950	07:53	16:30	05:55	18:30	00:10	10:27	
22	W	John Hurt b. 1940	07:52	16:32	06:31	19:11	01:22	10:39	
23	Th	Shensi earthquake 1556	07:50	16:34	07:17	20:04	02:36	10:56	
24	F	Winston Churchill d. 1965	07:49	16:36	08:29	21:15	03:51	11:19	
25	Sa	Burns Night	07:48	16:37	09:59	22:28	05:05	11:52	
26	Su	Australia Day	07:47	16:39	11:10	23:38	06:12	12:39	
27	M	Holocaust Memorial Day	07:45	16:41	—	12:12	07:06	13:45	
28	Tu	Diet of Worms op. 1521	07:44	16:43	00:38	13:05	07:45	15:04	
29	W	Chinese New Year (Snake)	07:42	16:44	01:28	13:57	08:13	16:29	
30	Th	Anton Checkhov b. 1860	07:41	16:46	02:12	14:36	08:33	18:01	
31	F	Leon Trotsky exiled 1929	07:39	16:48	02:53	15:19	08:49	19:29	

MOON'S PHASES JANUARY 2025

		Days	Hours	Mins
☽	First Quarter	6	23	56
○	Full Moon	13	22	26
☾	Last Quarter	21	20	30
●	New Moon	29	12	35

All times on this page are GMT

PREDICTIONS

The Full Moon on 13 January falls in Cancer in a close conjunction with Mars in the tenth house and a harmonious sextile to Uranus. Venus is conjunct Saturn in the sixth at London. The mood of the times favours conflict over compromise. Individual groups will assert their rights and countries will follow their national interest. The British Navy may see action overseas. The British government could move to take strong action in reforming parliament and the electoral system. There may be changes to laws concerning property ownership. Overseas, there may be a significant challenge to the government in Russia, and signs of future discontent.

The New Moon on 29 January falls in Aquarius in a wide conjunction with Pluto in the ninth house. Travel plans are likely to be disrupted and international relations will be in a state of crisis. We might expect international treaties to combat organised crime as well as the exposure of criminal connections at the highest level of British society. The Chinese government is likely to institute reforms intended to gain public support. Economic markets continue in a generally upward trend.

A firm favourite could romp home at the Cheltenham New Year Meeting; the Warwick *Classic Handicap Chase* may be won by a 10-year-old carrying 10st 8lb.

Predicted political return of Netanyahu in Israel 2023

FEBRUARY

For High Water add 5h 30m for Bristol, 4h 23m for Hull, 0h 43m for Leith; subtract 2h 21m for Dublin, 1h 26m for Greenock, 2h 29m for Liverpool.

D of M	D of W	Festivals, Events and Anniversaries	Sun at London Rises	Sun at London Sets	High Water at London Bridge am	High Water at London Bridge pm	Moon at London Rises	Moon at London Sets	Weather
1	Sa	Edward III crowned 1327	07:38	16:50	03:32	16:00	09:02	20:55	A lively mix of weathers: gales at the first in many parts, mostly from north and west, giving way to brighter days although cold until mid-month. Milder to follow.
2	Su	Candlemas Day	07:36	16:52	04:10	16:41	09:14	22:21	
3	M	Wind of Change' speech 1960	07:35	16:54	04:48	17:23	09:27	23:49	
4	Tu	World Cancer Day	07:33	16:55	05:27	18:07	09:41	—	
5	W	Kirk Douglas d. 2020	07:32	16:57	06:10	18:56	10:00	01:17	
6	Th	King George VI d. 1952	07:30	16:59	07:02	19:55	10:25	02:46	
7	F	First Prince of Wales 1301	07:28	17:01	08:14	21:06	11:02	04:10	
8	Sa	James Dean b. 1931	07:26	17:03	09:40	22:27	11:55	05:23	
9	Su	Fyodor Dostoyevsky d. 1881	07:25	17:04	11:04	23:47	13:03	06:17	
10	M	New Delhi India capital 1931	07:23	17:06	—	12:18	14:22	06:55	
11	Tu	Thatcher Cons. leader 1975	07:21	17:08	00:48	13:14	15:43	07:21	
12	W	Dior's 'New Look' 1947	07:19	17:10	01:36	14:00	17:03	07:39	
13	Th	Rachel Reeves b. 1979	07:17	17:12	02:16	14:40	18:19	07:53	
14	F	St Valentine	07:15	17:14	02:52	15:17	19:32	08:04	
15	Sa	UK decimalisation 1971	07:13	17:15	03:24	15:49	20:44	08:14	
16	Su	Castro Cuban leader 1959	07:12	17:17	03:54	16:19	21:54	08:23	
17	M	Jefferson US Pres. 1801	07:10	17:19	04:24	16:47	23:06	08:33	
18	Tu	Duke of Clarence ex. 1478	07:08	17:21	04:53	17:16	—	08:45	
19	W	Nicolaus Copernicus b. 1473	07:06	17:23	05:22	17:45	00:18	08:59	
20	Th	Edward VI crowned 1547	07:04	17:25	05:53	18:19	01:33	09:19	
21	F	John Thaw d. 2002	07:02	17:26	06:32	19:03	02:47	09:46	
22	Sa	Julie Walters b. 1950	07:00	17:28	07:25	20:03	03:56	10:26	
23	Su	Dame Nellie Melba b. 1931	06:57	17:30	08:54	21:38	04:55	11:22	
24	M	Penny Red released 1854	06:55	17:32	10:33	23:05	05:40	12:35	
25	Tu	Ed Balls b. 1967	06:53	17:34	11:44	—	06:13	13:59	
26	W	Fanny Cradock b. 1909	06:51	17:35	00:12	12:43	06:36	15:28	
27	Th	Labour Party founded 1900	06:49	17:37	01:05	13:32	06:54	16:58	
28	F	Ramadan begins	06:47	17:39	01:50	14:17	07:08	18:28	

MOON'S PHASES FEBRUARY 2025

		Days	Hours	Mins
☽ First Quarter		5	08	02
○ Full Moon		12	13	53
☾ Last Quarter		20	17	32
● New Moon		28	00	44

All times on this page are GMT

PREDICTIONS

The Full Moon on 12 February is in Leo on the third house cusp in a dynamic T-square with the Sun, Mercury and Uranus. Educational reforms top the agenda with a shake-up of the exam system and new regulation of universities on the cards. The government is likely to be afflicted by a lack of direction and will be accused of announcing redundant or somewhat odd policies upon which they do not follow through. Economic pressures mount in China which is entering a long period of internal tension. The Iranian government will most likely take strong action to silence its critics after a fresh round of protests.

The New Moon on 28 February falls in Pisces in the third house. Uranus is setting at London indicating the need for a reset of foreign policy. There may be heavy floods across the UK and the water infrastructure could buckle under the strain. The housing shortage hits critical levels. Global attentions peak in Southeast Asia and both Myanmar and Thailand face radical changes of government. NATO is in a confident and expansive mood, ready to meet military challenges. The financial situation remains confident, with dips in the market being short-lived.

The Betfair *Ascot Chase* may be won by a 10-year-old, while Newbury's Betfair *Hurdle* may see a 7-year-old carrying 11st 2lb as victor.

Predicted division and factions in Conservative Party 2024

MARCH

For High Water add 5h 30m for Bristol, 4h 23m for Hull, 0h 43m for Leith; subtract 2h 21m for Dublin, 1h 26m for Greenock, 2h 29m for Liverpool.

D of M	D of W	Festivals, Events and Anniversaries	Sun at London		High Water at London Bridge		Moon at London		Weather
			Rises	Sets	am	pm	Rises	Sets	
			h m	h m	h m	h m	h m	h m	
1	Sa	St David's Day	06:45	17:41	02:32	15:00	07:20	19:57	A hint of early spring with generally settled and fine weather throughout the month, although cold at night with some rain expected in the north and west.
2	Su	First £1 note 1797	06:43	17:42	03:12	15:41	07:33	21:27	
3	M	Apollo 9 launch 1969	06:40	17:44	03:50	16:21	07:47	22:59	
4	Tu	Shrove Tuesday	06:38	17:46	04:29	17:01	08:05	—	
5	W	Ash Wednesday	06:36	17:48	05:09	17:43	08:28	00:31	
6	Th	World Book Day	06:34	17:49	05:53	18:28	09:01	01:59	
7	F	Ranulph Fiennes b. 1933	06:32	17:51	06:46	19:23	09:49	03:16	
8	Sa	Int. Women's Day	06:29	17:53	07:57	20:37	10:53	04:16	
9	Su	First Sunday in Lent	06:27	17:55	09:25	22:09	12:08	04:58	
10	M	Long Beach earthquake 1933	06:25	17:56	10:55	23:32	13:28	05:27	
11	Tu	Commonwealth Day	06:23	17:58	—	12:07	14:48	05:46	
12	W	Liza Minnelli b. 1946	06:20	18:00	00:31	13:00	16:04	06:01	
13	Th	Feast of St Roderick	06:18	18:01	01:16	13:42	17:18	06:13	
14	F	Holi/Lunar eclipse 03 57	06:16	18:03	01:54	14:19	18:29	06:22	
15	Sa	Julius Caesar ass. 44 BC	06:14	18:05	02:27	14:51	19:40	06:32	
16	Su	New Eng. Bible pub. 1970	06:11	18:07	02:57	15:20	20:51	06:41	
17	M	St Patrick's Day	06:09	18:08	03:26	15:46	22:03	06:52	
18	Tu	Vesuvius erupts 1944	06:07	18:10	03:55	16:13	23:17	07:05	
19	W	Arthur C Clarke d. 2008	06:05	18:12	04:24	16:41	—	07:22	
20	Th	Spring equinox 09 01	06:02	18:13	04:53	17:10	00:31	07:46	
21	F	Thomas Cranmer exec. 1556	06:00	18:15	05:25	17:43	01:42	08:20	
22	Sa	A. Lloyd Webber b. 1948	05:58	18:17	06:04	18:25	02:45	09:08	
23	Su	Roger Bannister b. 1929	05:56	18:18	06:55	19:21	03:35	10:12	
24	M	Lord Alan Sugar b. 1947	05:53	18:20	08:10	20:48	04:11	11:30	
25	Tu	Henry II b. 1133	05:51	18:22	09:56	22:28	04:38	12:55	
26	W	Leonard Nimoy b. 1931	05:49	18:24	11:12	23:39	04:57	14:23	
27	Th	Charles I King 1625	05:46	18:25	—	12:14	05:12	15:52	
28	F	Paul O'Grady d. 2023	05:44	18:27	00:34	13:05	05:26	17:22	
29	Sa	Solar eclipse (part) 08 50	05:42	18:29	01:22	13:52	05:38	18:53	
30	Su	Mothering Sunday	05:40	18:30	02:05	14:35	05:52	20:27	
31	M	Eid-al Fitr	05:37	18:32	02:47	15:17	06:08	22:03	

MOON'S PHASES MARCH 2025

		Days	Hours	Mins
☽	First Quarter	6	16	31
○	Full Moon	14	06	54
☾	Last Quarter	22	11	29
●	New Moon	29	10	57

All times on this page are GMT (Add 1 hr DST from 30th)

PREDICTIONS

The Full Moon on 14 March is an eclipse and falls in Virgo on the sixth house in London in a harmonious trine with Uranus. Saturn is conjunct the Sun in the twelfth. The mental health crisis causes major strains in the NHS, and there is a need for innovatory financial solutions. There are fresh fears of espionage and a spy ring in the government. The Baltic states enter a critical period with a risk of conflict. Southern Africa is experiencing financial pressures and Zambia and Zimbabwe could require an international bail-out. In Egypt, Colombia and Venezuela tensions may rise.

The New Moon on 29 March is an eclipse in Aries in the tenth house at London. Saturn is in the Midheaven, and Mars is on the ascendant. The best laid government plans misfire and its popularity may drop significantly. There is a pressing need to build up the Navy and deep concerns about technological failures in the armed forces generally. The EU will be in a state of transformation with national governments asserting their rights over the bureaucracy. Changes in the Algerian government promote plans for greater stability in the Mediterranean.

The *Imperial Cup Handicap Hurdle* at Sandown may see a 4-year-old carrying 10st 2lb as winner, while the *Cheltenham Gold Cup* may be won by an 8-year-old favourite.

Predicted outbreak of World War II

APRIL

For High Water add 5h 30m for Bristol, 4h 23m for Hull, 0h 43m for Leith; subtract 2h 21m for Dublin, 1h 26m for Greenock, 2h 29m for Liverpool.

D of M	D of W	Festivals, Events and Anniversaries	Sun at London Rises	Sun at London Sets	High Water at London Bridge am	High Water at London Bridge pm	Moon at London Rises	Moon at London Sets	Weather
			h m	h m	h m	h m	h m	h m	
1	Tu	April Fool's Day	05:35	18:34	03:28	15:58	06:29	23:37	
2	W	Penelope Keith b. 1939	05:33	18:35	04:10	16:39	06:59	—	
3	Th	Prince Rainier d. 2005	05:30	18:37	04:53	17:20	07:43	01:02	
4	F	M. Luther King assass. 1968	05:28	18:39	05:39	18:05	08:43	02:11	
5	Sa	Churchill resigns 1955	05:26	18:40	06:35	18:59	09:57	02:59	Although initially changeable at the start and with mid-month rain, the weather works towards improvement with a more settled sunny spell at the close.
6	Su	Sir John Betjeman b. 1906	05:24	18:42	07:46	20:14	11:17	03:32	
7	M	Hatton Garden heist 2015	05:22	18:44	09:08	21:43	12:36	03:54	
8	Tu	Betty Ford b. 1918	05:19	18:45	10:31	23:03	13:53	04:09	
9	W	Charles m. Camilla 2005	05:17	18:47	11:42	—	15:07	04:22	
10	Th	*Great Gatsby* pub. 1925	05:15	18:49	00:02	12:34	16:18	04:32	
11	F	Roger Mortimer b. 1374	05:13	18:50	00:47	13:15	17:29	04:41	
12	Sa	Passover begins	05:11	18:52	01:25	13:50	18:39	04:51	
13	Su	Palm Sunday	05:08	18:54	01:58	14:20	19:51	05:01	
14	M	Henry I b. 1204	05:06	18:55	02:28	14:48	21:04	05:13	
15	Tu	Johnson's Dictionary pub. 1755	05:04	18:57	02:58	15:14	22:18	05:29	
16	W	Charlie Chaplin b. 1889	05:02	18:59	03:28	15:42	23:30	05:50	
17	Th	Maundy Thursday	05:00	19:00	03:58	16:12	—	06:20	
18	F	Good Friday	04:58	19:02	04:31	16:43	00:36	07:03	
19	Sa	Rainier m. G Kelly 1956	04:56	19:04	05:06	17:18	01:30	08:00	
20	Su	Easter Day/P'over ends	04:53	19:05	05:47	18:01	02:10	09:11	
21	M	Easter Monday	04:51	19:07	06:40	18:57	02:39	10:31	
22	T	Earth Day	04:49	19:09	07:51	20:15	03:01	11:56	
23	W	St George/Pr Louis b. 2018	04:47	19:10	09:23	21:49	03:17	13:21	
24	Th	Estée Lauder d. 2004	04:45	19:12	10:37	23:01	03:31	14:48	
25	F	Anzac Day	04:43	19:14	11:40	—	03:43	16:17	
26	Sa	Melania Trump b. 1970	04:41	19:15	00:00	12:35	03:56	17:48	
27	Su	Low Sunday	04:39	19:17	00:51	13:24	04:11	19:23	
28	M	Mutiny on the Bounty 1789	04:37	19:19	01:38	14:10	04:29	21:01	
29	Tu	P William m. Catherine 2011	04:35	19:20	02:23	14:53	04:55	22:34	
30	W	Hawaii a US state 1900	04:33	19:22	03:08	15:36	05:34	23:54	

PREDICTIONS

The Full Moon on 13 April falls in Libra, on the Midheaven at London in a challenging T-square with Mars and the Sun and a creative 'kite' formation with Venus, Saturn and Uranus. The mood is very tense and volatile but the time is ripe for creating new and lasting solutions to long-standing problems. Travel plans are likely to be disrupted and shipping lanes will be blocked. The west coast of North America faces a risk of earth tremors and serious damage to infrastructure. Pressures in central Asia could easily rise with the risk of neighbours being drawn into a much renewed Afghan conflict.

The New Moon on 27 April falls in Aries and the sixth house at London in a volcanic T-square with Mars and Pluto. Uranus, the planet of sudden change, is in a difficult square with Saturn and Venus. This signifies a turning point in world affairs although the implications will take months to become clear. Governments should re-double their peacekeeping efforts and focus on compromise to prevent conflict spreading. The Indian government forms new international alliances, attempting to become an Asian superpower. A military coup or wider conflict is possible in Nigeria.

At Aintree's *Grand National* a 9-year-old modestly backed horse may be a surprise winner; the *Scottish Grand National* may likewise go to a 9-year-old.

MOON'S PHASES APRIL 2025

		Days	Hours	Mins
☽	First Quarter	5	02	14
○	Full Moon	13	12	22
☾	Last Quarter	21	01	35
●	New Moon	27	19	31

All times on this page are GMT (Add 1 hr DST)

Predicted resolution of Northern Ireland Assembly, February 2024

MAY

For High Water add 5h 30m for Bristol, 4h 23m for Hull, 0h 43m for Leith; subtract 2h 21m for Dublin, 1h 26m for Greenock, 2h 29m for Liverpool.

D of M	D of W	Festivals, Events and Anniversaries	Sun at London Rises	Sun at London Sets	High Water at London Bridge am	High Water at London Bridge pm	Moon at London Rises	Moon at London Sets	Weather
			h m	h m	h m	h m	h m	h m	
1	Th	Alexandra Palace reopen 1875	04:32	19:24	03:53	16:19	06:28	—	A typical spring month with sun, rain and light winds but one that also delivers an extension of sunny days and a good start to the holiday season. Warm at the close.
2	F	Princess Charlotte b. 2015	04:30	19:25	04:40	17:02	07:40	00:53	
3	Sa	Eiffel Tower opened 1889	04:28	19:27	05:29	17:48	09:01	01:32	
4	Su	Margaret Thatcher PM 1979	04:26	19:28	06:25	18:41	10:23	01:58	
5	M	May Day bank holiday	04:24	19:30	07:30	19:49	11:42	02:16	
6	Tu	Prince Archie b. 2019	04:23	19:32	08:40	21:06	12:57	02:30	
7	W	Robert Browning b. 1812	04:21	19:33	09:52	22:17	14:09	02:41	
8	Th	VE Day 1945	04:19	19:35	11:00	23:18	15:19	02:50	
9	F	JM Barrie b. 1860	04:17	19:36	11:55	—	16:29	03:00	
10	Sa	Fred Astaire b. 1899	04:16	19:38	00:08	12:38	17:40	03:10	
11	Su	Siam became Thailand 1949	04:14	19:40	00:49	13:15	18:53	03:21	
12	M	Vesak Day	04:13	19:41	01:26	13:48	20:07	03:36	
13	Tu	Daphne du Maurier b. 1907	04:11	19:43	02:01	14:18	21:20	03:56	
14	W	Eric Morecambe b. 1926	04:09	19:44	02:33	14:47	22:28	04:23	
15	Th	Andy Murray b. 1987	04:08	19:46	03:05	15:18	23:25	05:02	
16	F	Nylon stockings on sale 1940	04:07	19:47	03:39	15:51	—	05:55	
17	Sa	Edward Jenner b. 1749	04:05	19:49	04:15	16:27	00:09	07:01	
18	Su	UN moves to NYC 1951	04:04	19:50	04:55	17:05	00:42	08:18	
19	M	Martin Amis d. 2023	04:02	19:52	05:39	17:49	01:05	09:39	
20	Tu	Robin Gibb d. 2012	04:01	19:53	06:31	18:42	01:22	11:02	
21	W	Elizabeth Fry b. 1780	04:00	19:54	07:36	19:48	01:36	12:25	
22	Th	Wright aeroplane patent 1906	03:58	19:56	08:53	21:12	01:49	13:49	
23	F	Bonnie and Clyde killed 1934	03:57	19:57	10:04	22:25	02:01	15:16	
24	Su	Tina Turner d. 2023	03:56	19:58	11:07	23:27	02:14	16:47	
25	Su	Rogation Sunday	03:55	20:00	—	12:06	02:31	18:22	
26	M	Spring bank holiday	03:54	20:01	00:23	12:59	02:52	19:58	
27	Tu	Anthony Eden PM 1955	03:53	20:02	01:15	13:47	03:24	21:26	
28	W	Lord Haw Haw captured 1945	03:52	20:03	02:04	14:34	04:11	22:37	
29	Th	Ascension Day	03:51	20:05	02:52	15:19	05:17	23:26	
30	F	First car accident 1896	03:50	20:06	03:41	16:04	06:37	23:58	
31	Sa	Battle of Jutland 1916	03:49	20:07	04:30	16:48	08:01	—	

PREDICTIONS

The Full Moon on 12 May falls In Scorpio on the second house cusp at London and a harmonious trine to Saturn. The international monetary situation may be subject to a series of shocks, but this is a positive moment for shrewd investors who can spot a bargain. The oil and shipping industries may prove to be good investments. There will be new attempts to ban over exploitation of the sea. Tensions rise in Central America with pressure for social reform in Nicaragua and Honduras. Angola experiences a boom thanks to increased oil production. Vietnam climbs up the ranks of prosperous East Asian countries and the Japanese economy will be entering a new era of growth.

The New Moon on 27 May falls in Gemini close to the second cusp at London and in a harmonious trine with Pluto. Saturn is conjunct Neptune in the twelfth house at London. There may be announcements of major new funding for schools, transport and communications projects, including railways and satellite networks. Worries about the future are offset by a sense that this is the time to make dreams come true. Concerns about espionage at the heart of government intensify. Strategic pressures in Europe focus on a change of government in Serbia.

The *1,000* and *2,000 Guineas* at Newmarket may see second favourites winning – the latter perhaps even by an outsider.

MOON'S PHASES MAY 2025

		Days	Hours	Mins
☽	First Quarter	4	13	51
○	Full Moon	12	16	55
☾	Last Quarter	20	11	58
●	New Moon	27	03	02

All times on this page are GMT (Add 1 hr DST)

Predicted launch of the Euro, January 2002

JUNE

For High Water add 5h 30m for Bristol, 4h 23m for Hull, 0h 43m for Leith; subtract 2h 21m for Dublin, 1h 26m for Greenock, 2h 29m for Liverpool.

D of M	D of W	Festivals, Events and Anniversaries	Sun at London Rises	Sun at London Sets	High Water at London Bridge am	High Water at London Bridge pm	Moon at London Rises	Moon at London Sets	Weather
			h m	h m	h m	h m	h m	h m	
1	Su	Shavuot begins	03:48	20:08	05:19	17:32	09:24	12:20	
2	M	PT Barnum's circus op. 1835	03:48	20:09	06:11	18:20	10:42	12:36	
3	Tu	Shavuot ends	03:47	20:10	07:06	19:16	11:57	12:48	
4	W	Princess Lilibet b. 2021	03:46	20:11	08:04	20:20	13:08	12:58	
5	Th	EEC referendum 1975	03:46	20:12	09:03	21:24	14:18	01:08	While conditions are changeable in the north, there should be some settled, fine, warmer days throughout the month especially in the Midlands, east and south.
6	F	D-Day 1944	03:45	20:13	10:02	22:24	15:29	01:18	
7	Sa	*Lusitania* launched 1906	03:45	20:14	11:00	23:21	16:41	01:29	
8	Su	Pentecost	03:44	20:15	11:53	—	17:54	01:42	
9	M	Iain Banks d. 2013	03:44	20:15	00:11	12:38	19:08	02:00	
10	Tu	Duke of Edinburgh b. 1921	03:43	20:16	00:56	13:17	20:18	02:25	
11	W	John Aspinall b. 1927	03:43	20:17	01:37	13:54	21:20	03:00	
12	Th	Insulin patented 1922	03:43	20:17	02:14	14:29	22:08	03:49	
13	F	WB Yeats b. 1865	03:43	20:18	02:51	15:04	22:44	04:53	
14	Sa	Trooping the Colour	03:42	20:19	03:28	15:40	23:10	06:08	
15	Su	Trinity/Father's Day	03:42	20:19	04:06	16:18	23:28	07:28	
16	M	*Psycho* opens NYC 1960	03:42	20:20	04:47	16:57	23:43	08:50	
17	Tu	Drake lands in US 1579	03:42	20:20	05:31	17:38	23:56	10:12	
18	W	Titan sub implodes 2023	03:42	20:20	06:20	18:25	—	11:34	
19	Th	Corpus Christi	03:42	20:21	07:17	19:21	00:07	12:57	
20	F	Errol Flynn b. 1909	03:42	20:21	08:24	20:34	00:20	14:23	
21	Sa	Solstice 03 41/Pr Wm b. 1982	03:43	20:21	09:32	21:51	00:34	15:53	
22	Su	Prunella Scales b. 1932	03:43	20:21	10:37	22:59	00:53	17:26	
23	M	Nasser Egypt president 1956	03:43	20:21	11:41	—	01:19	18:57	
24	Tu	Jack Dempsey b. 1895	03:44	20:21	00:02	12:39	01:57	20:16	
25	W	Islamic New Year begins	03:44	20:21	00:59	13:32	02:54	21:15	
26	Th	V&A Museum opened 1909	03:44	20:21	01:52	14:20	04:08	21:55	
27	F	Central Line opened 1900	03:45	20:21	02:43	15:06	05:33	22:21	
28	Sa	UK Armed Forces Day	03:45	20:21	03:32	15:50	06:59	22:40	
29	Su	Globe Theatre fire 1613	03:46	20:21	04:19	16:32	08:22	22:53	
30	M	Stanley Spencer b. 1891	03:47	20:21	05:04	17:12	09:39	23:05	

MOON'S PHASES JUNE 2025

		Days	Hours	Mins
☽	First Quarter	3	03	40
○	Full Moon	11	07	43
☾	Last Quarter	18	19	19
●	New Moon	25	10	31

All times on this page are GMT (Add 1 hr DST)

PREDICTIONS

The Full Moon on 11 June is in Sagittarius in the fifth house at London. There is a challenging T-square between Jupiter, Mercury Saturn and Neptune. This is a time to think big and to make dreams come true by combining a vision of a better future with an understanding of the need for clear and detailed practical plans. If the will is present then the foundations may be laid for a much better and stronger world during the coming decades, but governments need to avoid any tendency to muddle and confusion. International hotspots include Greece, which is facing a phase of political renewal.

The New Moon on 25 June falls in Cancer in the tenth house at London in an exact conjunction with Jupiter and a square to Saturn and Neptune. There is a risk that governments will overreach themselves and undertake rash actions that they are unable to complete, exacerbating existing problems. A focus on hard work and practical measures is vital at this time. Europe is a potential conflict zone and measures to create trust and open dialogue rather than confrontation must be the top priority for the regions' governments. South Africa is at a turning point and rival communities must work together to avoid a government meltdown.

The Epsom *Oaks* may go to a firm favourite, while the *Derby* could be won by a jockey from northern England.

Predicted mass demonstrations in France 2023

  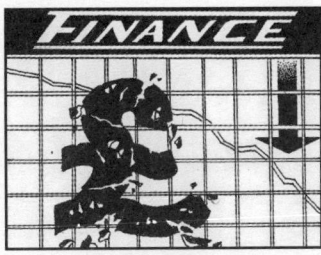

JULY

For High Water add 5h 30m for Bristol, 4h 23m for Hull, 0h 43m for Leith; subtract 2h 21m for Dublin, 1h 26m for Greenock, 2h 29m for Liverpool.

D of M	D of W	Festivals, Events and Anniversaries	Sun at London Rises	Sun at London Sets	High Water at London Bridge am	High Water at London Bridge pm	Moon at London Rises	Moon at London Sets	Weather
			h m	h m	h m	h m	h m	h m	
1	Tu	Princess Diana b. 1961	03:47	20:20	05:47	17:51	10:53	23:15	
2	W	Live 8 concert 2005	03:48	20:20	06:31	18:33	12:04	23:24	
3	Th	Tom Cruise b. 1962	03:49	20:19	07:16	19:23	13:15	23:35	
4	F	US Independence Day	03:50	20:19	08:06	20:24	14:27	23:48	
5	Sa	Ashe wins Wimbledon 1975	03:50	20:18	09:00	21:28	15:40	—	
6	Su	Nancy Reagan b. 1921	03:51	20:18	09:58	22:31	16:54	00:04	From a thundery start, a progression to clearer, brighter days will bring the spirit of summer relaxation until near the close, when thundery conditions return.
7	M	7/7 terrorist attacks 2005	03:52	20:17	11:00	23:32	18:06	00:26	
8	Tu	Biggs escapes jail 1965	03:53	20:17	11:59	—	19:11	00:57	
9	W	Sir Edward Heath b. 1916	03:54	20:16	00:28	12:51	20:05	01:42	
10	Th	William of Orange ass. 1584	03:55	20:15	01:16	13:35	20:45	02:41	
11	F	Waterloo Station op. 1848	03:56	20:14	01:59	14:16	21:14	03:54	
12	Sa	Orangemen's Day (hol) NI	03:57	20:13	02:39	14:54	21:34	05:14	
13	Su	Ruth Ellis hanged 1955	03:58	20:13	03:19	15:31	21:50	06:38	
14	M	Bastille Day (France)	04:00	20:12	03:58	16:08	22:03	08:00	
15	Tu	St Swithin's Day	04:01	20:11	04:37	16:44	22:15	09:23	
16	W	Potsdam conference 1945	04:02	20:10	05:18	17:23	22:27	10:45	
17	Th	HM Queen Camilla b. 1947	04:03	20:09	06:02	18:05	22:40	12:09	
18	F	Nelson Mandela b. 1918	04:04	20:07	06:52	18:55	22:57	13:36	
19	Sa	James Garner d. 2014	04:06	20:06	07:51	19:59	23:19	15:06	
20	Su	First moon landing 1969	04:07	20:05	08:59	21:22	23:51	16:36	
21	M	Battle of Shrewsbury 1403	04:08	20:04	10:10	22:38	—	17:58	
22	Tu	Prince George b. 2013	04:10	20:02	11:22	23:50	00:39	19:04	
23	W	Ford sells first car 1903	04:11	20:01	—	12:28	01:45	19:51	
24	Th	Speaking clock beg. 1936	04:12	20:00	00:54	13:23	03:06	20:22	
25	F	Islamic New Year	04:14	19:58	01:48	14:11	04:32	20:43	
26	Sa	Attlee PM 1945	04:15	19:57	02:36	14:53	05:57	20:59	
27	Su	Heath Cons. leader 1965	04:17	19:56	03:20	15:33	07:17	21:11	
28	M	J Kennedy Onassis b. 1929	04:18	19:54	04:01	16:10	08:33	21:21	
29	Tu	Joey Essex b. 1990	04:20	19:52	04:39	16:44	09:47	21:31	
30	W	England win World Cup 1966	04:21	19:51	05:15	17:17	10:59	21:42	
31	Th	Columbus lands Trinidad 1498	04:23	19:49	05:48	17:50	12:11	21:53	

MOON'S PHASES JULY 2025

		Days	Hours	Mins
☽	First Quarter	2	19	30
○	Full Moon	10	20	36
☾	Last Quarter	18	12	37
●	New Moon	24	19	11

All times on this page are GMT (Add 1 hr DST)

PREDICTIONS

The Full Moon on 10 July falls in Capricorn in a square with the UK Moon. Jupiter is opposed the UK Midheaven and is taking on a critical role in world affairs. We are entering a new phase of optimism and hope for the future. The emphasis should be on balancing the powers of different regions of the UK and devolving powers to those regions. The financial situation is unstable and there is a need to deal with high levels of debt. The amount of energy generated by renewables will increase dramatically. Germany, France and the USA are all entering an expansive period, taking on new international responsibilities and experiencing economic growth.

The New Moon on 24 July falls in Leo in the seventh house at London, and in an exact opposition with Pluto. The general mood is highly volatile with people and governments preferring to apportion blame upon each other rather than seeking solutions. The financial situation remains highly unstable so sensible investors should avoid risk. Prospects for a new peace treaty between Israel and its neighbours are high. Libya reaches a major new agreement with the EU to restrict the flow of refugees. Earth tremors are likely at this time in California.

The Ascot *International Stakes* may go to a 4-year-old carrying 10st 5lb. Newmarket's *Darley July Cup* could see a 1-year-old carrying 9st 2lb as winner.

Predicted bomb on Hiroshima 1945

AUGUST

For High Water add 5h 30m for Bristol, 4h 23m for Hull, 0h 43m for Leith; subtract 2h 21m for Dublin, 1h 26m for Greenock, 2h 29m for Liverpool.

D of M	D of W	Festivals, Events and Anniversaries	Sun at London Rises	Sun at London Sets	High Water at London Bridge am	High Water at London Bridge pm	Moon at London Rises	Moon at London Sets	Wea-ther
			h m	h m	h m	h m	h m	h m	
1	F	Cilla Black d. 2015	04:24	19:48	06:22	18:25	13:24	22:08	
2	Sa	Gainsborough d. 1788	04:26	19:46	07:01	19:10	14:37	22:27	
3	Su	Rupert Brooke b. 1887	04:27	19:44	07:50	20:22	15:51	22:54	
4	M	Bank holiday (Scotland)	04:29	19:43	08:57	21:44	16:59	23:33	
5	Tu	Sir Bob Geldof b. 1951	04:30	19:41	10:11	22:56	17:57	—	
6	W	Alfred Lord Tennyson b. 1809	04:32	19:39	11:24	—	18:43	00:26	
7	Th	Litter Act in force 1958	04:33	19:37	00:00	12:25	19:15	01:34	
8	F	Roger Federer b. 1981	04:35	19:35	00:54	13:14	19:39	02:53	
9	Sa	Sharon Tate d. 1969	04:36	19:34	01:40	13:57	19:57	04:17	
10	Su	Feast of St Laurence	04:38	19:32	02:22	14:36	20:11	05:42	
11	M	Atlantic Charter 1941	04:39	19:30	03:02	15:14	20:23	07:07	
12	Tu	Cecil B. DeMille b. 1881	04:41	19:28	03:41	15:50	20:35	09:31	
13	W	John Logie Baird b. 1888	04:43	19:26	04:20	16:26	20:48	09:56	
14	Th	VJ Day 1945	04:44	19:24	04:59	17:03	21:03	11:23	
15	F	Princess Royal b. 1950	04:46	19:22	05:40	17:44	21:23	12:52	
16	Sa	Michael Parkinson d. 2023	04:47	19:20	06:25	18:32	21:51	14:22	
17	Su	*Animal Farm* pub. 1945	04:49	19:18	07:18	19:35	22:32	15:46	
18	M	Rosalynn Carter b. 1927	04:51	19:16	08:27	21:01	23:31	16:57	
19	Tu	John Dryden b. 1631	04:52	19:14	09:48	22:27	—	17:48	
20	W	Jamie Cullum b. 1979	04:54	19:12	11:13	23:47	00:45	18:24	
21	Th	Princess Margaret b. 1930	04:55	19:10	—	12:21	02:09	18:48	
22	F	Battle of Bosworth 1485	04:57	19:08	00:50	13:13	03:34	19:05	
23	Sa	Geoff Capes b. 1949	04:59	19:06	01:39	13:57	04:55	19:18	
24	Su	Stephen Fry b. 1957	05:00	19:03	02:22	14:35	06:13	19:29	
25	M	Bank holiday	05:02	19:01	03:00	15:09	07:28	19:39	
26	Tu	RAF bomb Berlin 1940	05:03	18:59	03:36	15:41	08:41	19:49	
27	W	Moldova independent 1991	05:05	18:57	04:08	16:12	09:54	20:00	
28	Th	Slavery Abolition Act 1833	05:07	18:55	04:37	16:42	11:06	20:13	
29	F	Ingrid Bergman b. 1915	05:08	18:53	05:05	17:12	12:20	20:30	
30	Sa	First trams ran 1860	05:10	18:50	05:33	17:42	13:34	20:53	
31	Su	Princess Diana d. 1997	05:11	18:48	06:04	18:19	14:44	21:26	

The poet's 'Burning August' is expected from the start until the third week, then closing with the threat of storms. Nevertheless, a satisfactory holiday month.

MOON'S PHASES AUGUST 2025

			Days	Hours	Mins
☽	First Quarter		1	12	41
○	Full Moon		9	07	55
☾	Last Quarter		16	05	12
●	New Moon		23	06	06
☽	First Quarter		31	06	25

All times on this page are GMT (Add 1 hr DST)

PREDICTIONS

The Full Moon on 9 August falls in Aquarius and the fifth house in London. There is an exact opposition between Mars, Saturn and Neptune. A 'splash' pattern between the planets brings both the choice and the ability to institute a wide raft of new reforms. The mood of the times is extremely volatile, and it is necessary that governments and people listen to each other and only act when the best interests of everybody concerned have been reconciled. There is still an emphasis on fossil fuel exploration, in spite of environmental concerns, and risks will be highlighted by accidents with oil pipelines and refineries.

The New Moon on 23 August falls in Virgo in the first house at London in an exact square with Uranus on the Midheaven. The government will be subject to unexpected shocks. There is a risk of the collapse of a major investment house and speculative investments are ill advised. Tension between the Baltic states and Russia intensifies. Italy, France and Germany enter a heightened level of co-operation at the heart of the EU. Venezuela and Colombia form a new economic alliance in South America which causes speculator's eyes to turn to the region.

This year's prestigious *King George Stakes* at Glorious Goodwood may see a 5-year-old horse carrying 8st 6lb as the winner. The *Ebor Handicap* at York may go to a 7-year-old horse carrying 9st 2lb.

Predicted war between Israel and Palestine in 2023

SEPTEMBER

For High Water add 5h 30m for Bristol, 4h 23m for Hull, 0h 43m for Leith; subtract 2h 21m for Dublin, 1h 26m for Greenock, 2h 29m for Liverpool.

D of M	D of W	Festivals, Events and Anniversaries	Sun at London Rises	Sun at London Sets	High Water at London Bridge am	High Water at London Bridge pm	Moon at London Rises	Moon at London Sets	Weather
			h m	h m	h m	h m	h m	h m	
1	M	Evac. of Atlanta 1864	05:13	18:46	06:44	19:10	15:47	22:12	
2	Tu	Great Fire of London 1666	05:15	18:44	07:41	20:43	16:37	23:14	Weather patterns are spread more evenly across the country from northern moors to southern coast with sunny days dominating the overall picture.
3	W	Merchant Navy Day	05:16	18:41	09:18	22:18	17:15	—	
4	Th	Joan Rivers d. 2014	05:18	18:39	10:47	23:28	17:42	00:28	
5	F	Napolean loses Malta 1800	05:19	18:37	11:54	—	18:01	01:50	
6	Sa	Liz Truss PM 2022	05:21	18:35	00:25	12:46	18:17	03:15	
7	Su	Lunar eclipse 15 28	05:22	18:32	01:13	13:30	18:30	04:41	
8	M	Access. Charles III 2022	05:24	18:30	01:57	14:10	18:42	06:07	
9	Tu	Leo Tolstoy b. 1828	05:26	18:28	02:38	14:49	18:55	07:34	
10	W	William Bligh b. 1754	05:27	18:26	03:18	15:27	19:09	09:03	
11	Th	9/11 2001	05:29	18:23	03:57	16:05	19:28	10:35	
12	F	Saragarhi Day	05:30	18:21	04:36	16:43	19:53	12:07	
13	Sa	World Athletics Ch. Op	05:32	18:19	05:16	17:26	20:30	13:35	
14	Su	Feast of the Cross	05:34	18:16	05:59	18:16	21:23	14:51	
15	M	Prince Harry b. 1984	05:35	18:14	06:50	19:21	22:33	15:48	
16	Tu	Henry V b. 1386	05:37	18:12	08:01	20:50	23:54	16:27	
17	W	Billy the Kid b. 1859	05:38	18:09	09:33	22:18	—	16:53	
18	Th	Tiffany & Co. op. 1837	05:40	18:07	10:59	23:37	01:17	17:12	
19	F	Funeral of Elizabeth II 2022	05:42	18:05	—	12:04	02:39	17:26	
20	Sa	Marc Bolan d. 1977	05:43	18:03	00:35	12:54	03:57	17:37	
21	Su	Solar eclipse 17 29	05:45	18:00	01:21	13:34	05:12	17:47	
22	M	Autumn eq. 19 19/Rosh H beg.	05:46	17:58	02:00	14:09	06:25	17:57	
23	Tu	Int. Sign Language Day	05:48	17:56	02:34	14:40	07:37	18:08	
24	W	Rosh Hashanah ends	05:50	17:53	03:05	15:10	08:50	18:20	
25	Th	Ronnie Barker b. 1929	05:51	17:51	03:33	15:40	10:04	18:35	
26	F	Fish fingers on sale 1955	05:53	17:49	04:00	16:10	11:18	18:56	
27	Sa	Michael Gambon d. 2023	05:54	17:46	04:27	16:40	12:29	19:20	
28	Su	Brigitte Bardot b. 1934	05:56	17:44	04:54	17:10	13:35	20:04	
29	M	Michaelmas	05:58	17:42	05:24	17:47	14:29	20:58	
30	Tu	*Magic Flute* debuts 1791	05:59	17:40	06:03	18:36	15:11	22:06	

MOON'S PHASES SEPTEMBER 2025

		Days	Hours	Mins
○	Full Moon	7	18	08
☽	Last Quarter	14	10	32
●	New Moon	21	19	54
☾	First Quarter	29	23	53

All times on this page are GMT (Add 1 hr DST)

PREDICTIONS

The Full Moon on 7 September falls in Pisces in the first house at London, in an opposition to Mercury and a harmonious trine to Jupiter. There is an atmosphere of goodwill and willingness to listen to what people want and what countries need. The search for peace remains a top priority in global relations. New laws will be enacted to protect the welfare of children and reinforce the role of the family. France experiences a period of political uncertainty and public protest, but the government will emerge stronger.

The New Moon on 21 September falls in Virgo on the sixth house cusp at London and in an opposition to Saturn and Neptune. Uranus is rising at London. Health matters are once again an overwhelming priority. There are fears of a new pandemic and huge problems caused by both physical and mental health problems. Innovative new solutions are required. The government may be hit by scandal and unexpected resignations. The USA is approaching a renewed period of public protest and polarisation. The Netherlands, Denmark and Norway are subject to renewal and reorganisation, and will work together to form a new bloc in Europe, protecting democratic values.

An Irish jockey may win the Doncaster *St. Leger*. At Ayr's *Gold Cup*, a 6-year-old carrying 9st 7lb may be victorious.

Predicted Margaret Thatcher's resignation 1990

OCTOBER

For High Water add 5h 30m for Bristol, 4h 23m for Hull, 0h 43m for Leith; subtract 2h 21m for Dublin, 1h 26m for Greenock, 2h 29m for Liverpool.

D of M	D of W	Festivals, Events and Anniversaries	Sun at London Rises	Sun at London Sets	High Water at London Bridge am	High Water at London Bridge pm	Moon at London Rises	Moon at London Sets	Weather
1	W	Yom Kippur	06:01	17:37	06:56	19:46	15:42	23:23	A sunny period during the first two weeks, calmer than usual for the time of year. Windy, with more traditional autumnal weather emerging at the close.
2	Th	First park run 2005	06:03	17:35	08:14	21:32	16:04	—	
3	F	Aerosol patent 1941	06:04	17:33	10:03	22:48	16:21	00:46	
4	Sa	Coverdale Bible pub. 1535	06:06	17:31	11:14	23:49	16:35	02:10	
5	Su	Love Me Do released 1962	06:08	17:28	—	12:09	16:48	04:36	
6	M	Sukkot begins	06:09	17:26	00:41	12:57	17:00	05:03	
7	Tu	Battle of Lepanto 1571	06:11	17:24	01:27	13:40	17:14	06:32	
8	W	Che Guevara captured 1967	06:13	17:22	02:10	14:22	17:31	08:05	
9	Th	David Cameron b. 1966	06:14	17:19	02:52	15:03	17:55	09:40	
10	F	World Mental Health Day	06:16	17:17	03:33	15:44	18:28	11:14	
11	Sa	Children's Hour began 1926	06:18	17:15	04:13	16:27	19:17	12:38	
12	Su	Brighton bombing 1984	06:19	17:13	04:54	17:13	20:23	13:43	
13	M	Sukkot ends	06:21	17:11	05:38	18:06	21:42	14:28	
14	Tu	Steve Cram b. 1960	06:23	17:08	06:30	19:14	23:05	14:58	
15	W	Great Storm 1987	06:24	17:06	07:41	20:36	—	15:19	
16	Th	Skye Bridge open 1995	06:26	17:04	09:11	21:57	00:27	15:34	
17	F	Rita Hayworth b. 1918	06:28	17:02	10:31	23:12	01:45	15:46	
18	Sa	San Fran. earthquake 1989	06:29	17:00	11:35	—	03:00	15:56	
19	Su	Jonathan Swift d. 1745	06:31	16:58	00:09	12:25	04:13	16:06	
20	M	Diwali	06:33	16:56	00:54	13:05	05:25	16:17	
21	Tu	B. Netanyahu b. 1949	06:35	16:54	01:31	13:40	06:37	16:28	
22	W	Paul Cezanne d. 1906	06:36	16:52	02:03	14:11	07:50	16:42	
23	Th	Ang Lee b. 1954	06:38	16:50	02:32	14:41	09:04	17:01	
24	F	United Nations Day	06:40	16:48	02:59	15:12	10:16	17:26	
25	Sa	Battle of Agincourt 1415	06:42	16:46	03:26	15:43	11:24	18:02	
26	Su	Hillary Clinton b. 1947	06:43	16:44	03:55	16:14	12:22	18:50	
27	M	John Cleese b. 1939	06:45	16:42	04:25	16:49	13:08	19:52	
28	Tu	Matthew Perry d. 2023	06:47	16:40	04:58	17:28	13:42	21:05	
29	W	Suez Crisis begins 1956	06:49	16:38	05:38	18:17	14:06	22:23	
30	Th	Henry VII crowned 1485	06:50	16:36	06:29	19:20	14:25	23:44	
31	F	Halloween	06:52	16:34	07:37	20:47	14:40	—	

PREDICTIONS

The Full Moon on 7 October is an eclipse in Aries in the eighth house at London. A 'splash' pattern encourages diversity, choice and the freedom to choose different directions. The focus is on the need for financial reform and protection of consumers. There is a general upward movement in the markets, although unnecessary risk should be avoided. Investment in luxury items, glamour, fashion and fantasy may bring long-term returns. There may be new experimental artistic movements emerging. Saudi Arabia takes the lead in new initiatives to establish peace and stability in the Middle East.

The New Moon on 21 October falls in Libra. Mars and Mercury are in conjunction and in a harmonious trine with Jupiter. The prevailing mood is one of 'can do' optimism and this is a positive moment to launch any new project. Property investments and house building are strong options. Social enterprises, which give back to the community, are strongly favoured. Tensions rise between India and Pakistan, but a lasting peace may be found if both sides are ready to compromise. The Horn of Africa is a focus of tension with Western navies in action.

The *Cesarewitch Heritage Handicap* may be won by a 4-year-old carrying 9st 8lb. The *Queen Elizabeth II Stakes* at Ascot may go to a 3-year-old carrying 8st 4lb.

MOON'S PHASES OCTOBER 2025		Days	Hours	Mins
○	Full Moon	7	03	47
☾	Last Quarter	14	10	32
●	New Moon	21	12	25
☽	First Quarter	29	16	20

All times on this page are GMT (DST to 26 October + 1 hour)

Predicted crisis for the SNP 2023-24

NOVEMBER

For High Water add 5h 30m for Bristol, 4h 23m for Hull, 0h 43m for Leith; subtract 2h 21m for Dublin, 1h 26m for Greenock, 2h 29m for Liverpool.

D of M	D of W	Festivals, Events and Anniversaries	Sun at London Rises	Sun at London Sets	High Water at London Bridge am	High Water at London Bridge pm	Moon at London Rises	Moon at London Sets	Weather
			h m	h m	h m	h m	h m	h m	
1	Sa	All Saints' Day	06:54	16:33	09:10	22:05	14:53	01:06	A mostly unsettled month with many changes of temperature. Some milder days at the start are followed by a significantly colder, wetter, windier period.
2	Su	Day of the Dead, Mexico	06:56	16:31	10:28	23:09	15:05	02:30	
3	M	Charles Bronson b. 1921	06:57	16:29	11:29	—	15:18	03:56	
4	Tu	Laura Bush b. 1946	06:59	16:27	00:05	12:22	15:33	05:26	
5	W	Bonfire Night	07:01	16:26	00:56	13:10	15:54	07:01	
6	Th	Nigel Havers b. 1949	07:03	16:24	01:42	13:57	16:23	08:39	
7	F	Lawrence Durrell d. 1948	07:04	16:22	02:27	14:42	17:05	10:11	
8	Sa	Death penalty abol. 1965	07:06	16:21	03:11	15:28	18:07	11:28	
9	Su	Remembrance Day	07:08	16:19	03:55	16:15	19:24	12:23	
10	M	Windows 1 launch 1983	07:10	16:18	04:39	17:05	20:50	12:59	
11	Tu	Armistice day 1918	07:11	16:16	05:24	17:59	22:14	13:24	
12	W	Grace Kelly b. 1929	07:13	16:15	06:15	19:03	23:35	13:41	
13	Th	Nell Gwynn d. 1687	07:15	16:13	07:21	20:12	—	13:54	
14	F	HM the King b. 1948	07:17	16:12	08:37	21:21	00:51	14:05	
15	Sa	Mantovani b. 1905	07:18	16:10	09:49	22:30	02:04	14:15	
16	Su	Henry III d. 1272	07:20	16:09	10:53	23:30	03:15	14:25	
17	M	International Students Day	07:22	16:08	11:46	—	04:26	14:36	
18	Tu	US military in Vietnam 1961	07:23	16:06	00:18	12:31	05:38	14:50	
19	W	King Charles I b. 1600	07:25	16:05	00:57	13:09	06:52	15:07	
20	Th	Pr Elizabeth m. Philip 1947	07:27	16:04	01:32	13:45	08:05	15:30	
21	F	René Magritte b. 1898	07:28	16:03	02:03	14:18	09:14	16:03	
22	Sa	JFK assassinated 1963	07:30	16:02	02:32	14:50	10:16	16:47	
23	Su	Larry Hagman d. 2012	07:32	16:01	03:02	15:23	11:05	17:45	
24	M	Billy Connolly b. 1942	07:33	16:00	03:34	15:57	11:42	18:54	
25	Tu	Terry Venables d. 2023	07:35	15:59	04:07	16:35	12:09	20:10	
26	W	Cyril Cusack b. 1910	07:36	15:58	04:44	17:16	12:29	21:28	
27	Th	Thanksgiving (USA)	07:38	15:57	05:24	18:04	12:45	22:47	
28	F	William Blake b. 1757	07:39	15:56	06:11	18:59	12:58	—	
29	Sa	George Harrison d. 2001	07:41	15:56	07:08	20:09	13:10	00:06	
30	Su	St Andrew/Advent beg.	07:42	15:55	08:19	21:24	13:22	01:28	

MOON'S PHASES NOVEMBER 2025		Days	Hours	Mins
	○ Full Moon	5	13	19
	☾ Last Quarter	12	05	28
	● New Moon	20	06	47
	☽ First Quarter	28	06	58

All times on this page are GMT

PREDICTIONS

The Full Moon on 5 November falls in Sagittarius on the third house cusp at London. Mercury is on the Midheaven. Education and training are overwhelming priorities with an emphasis on practical skills and international exchange. There is a strong sense that countries across the world are returning to the past and rediscovering former values and a pride in nationhood. There is also a revival of socialist principles and an awareness of the need to look after the most vulnerable. Russia is entering a period of great instability in its Asian republics, which may be countered by increased government control.

The New Moon on 20 November falls in Scorpio in an exact conjunction with Mercury and a tight opposition to Uranus. There is a grand trine with Jupiter, Saturn and Neptune. This is the second moment in the year when foundations are laid for large-scale political and technological developments over the next few decades. However, uncertainty returns, and the outcome of any government action is unclear. Foreign relations are in a state of volatility and former rivals may become allies. West Africa is under the spotlight and more countries will be taking the democratic path. Severe weather in the South Atlantic is likely.

In the Ladbroke's *Trophy Handicap* steeplechase a 4-year-old carrying exactly 10st may take the crown.

2026 Old Moore's Almanack on sale June 2025

DECEMBER

For High Water add 5h 30m for Bristol, 4h 23m for Hull, 0h 43m for Leith; subtract 2h 21m for Dublin, 1h 26m for Greenock, 2h 29m for Liverpool.

D of M	D of W	Festivals, Events and Anniversaries	Sun at London Rises	Sun at London Sets	High Water at London Bridge am	High Water at London Bridge pm	Moon at London Rises	Moon at London Sets	Weather
			h m	h m	h m	h m	h m	h m	
1	M	World AIDS Day	7:44	15:54	09:43	22:30	13:36	2:53	
2	Tu	Bhutto PM Pakistan 1988	7:45	15:54	10:51	23:31	13:53	4:22	
3	W	PlayStation released 1994	7:46	15:53	11:51	—	14:17	5:57	
4	Th	Thomas Carlyle b. 1795	7:48	15:53	00:27	12:46	14:52	7:33	
5	F	*Marie Celeste* found 1872	7:49	15:52	01:19	13:37	15:44	9:00	A very variable month with fluctuations in weather conditions across the country from week to week. A cold spell settling in before the close.
6	Sa	Feast of St Nicholas	7:50	15:52	02:08	14:27	16:57	10:08	
7	Su	B. Zephaniah d. 2023	7:51	15:52	02:55	15:17	18:23	10:54	
8	M	John Lennon murdered 1980	7:52	15:51	03:41	16:07	19:51	11:24	
9	Tu	*Coronation Street* began 1960	7:54	15:51	04:27	16:57	21:17	11:45	
10	W	Pneumatic tyre patent 1845	7:55	15:51	05:12	17:47	22:36	12:00	
11	Th	Willie Rushton d. 1996	7:56	15:51	05:58	18:41	23:52	12:12	
12	F	Kenya independent 1963	7:57	15:51	06:49	19:36	—	12:22	
13	Sa	Dick Van Dyke b. 1925	7:58	15:51	07:50	20:34	1:04	12:32	
14	Su	Jane Birkin b. 1946	7:58	15:51	08:55	21:33	2:16	12:43	
15	M	Tim Peake in space 2015	7:59	15:51	09:58	22:33	3:28	12:56	
16	Tu	Jane Austen b. 1775	8:00	15:51	10:58	23:31	4:41	13:12	
17	W	Tommy Steele b. 1936	8:01	15:51	11:52	—	5:54	13:34	
18	Th	Antonio Stradivari d. 1737	8:02	15:52	00:20	12:40	7:04	14:03	
19	F	Civil Partnership Act 2005	8:02	15:52	01:02	13:23	8:09	14:44	
20	Sa	Cardiff Welsh capital 1955	8:03	15:53	01:40	14:02	9:02	15:39	
21	Su	Winter solstice 15 32	8:03	15:53	02:15	14:37	9:43	16:45	
22	M	Lady Bird Johnson b. 1912	8:04	15:54	02:49	15:12	10:13	18:00	
23	Tu	Emperor Akihito b. 1933	8:04	15:54	03:23	15:48	10:35	19:17	
24	W	Christmas Eve	8:05	15:55	03:58	16:25	10:51	20:36	
25	Th	Christmas Day	8:05	15:55	04:34	17:06	11:05	21:54	
26	F	Boxing Day	8:05	15:56	05:12	17:49	11:17	23:12	
27	Sa	HMS *Beagle* sails 1831	8:05	15:57	05:53	18:37	11:28	—	
28	Su	Tay Bridge disaster 1879	8:06	15:58	06:41	19:34	11:41	0:33	
29	M	Thomas Becket assass. 1170	8:06	15:59	07:38	20:43	11:55	1:57	
30	Tu	Gordon Banks b. 1934	8:06	16:00	08:55	21:53	12:15	3:26	
31	W	New Year's Eve/Hogmanay	8:06	16:01	10:16	23:01	12:43	4:58	

MOON'S PHASES DECEMBER 2025			Days	Hours	Mins
	○	Full Moon	4	23	14
	☾	Last Quarter	11	20	51
	●	New Moon	20	01	43
	☽	First Quarter	27	19	09

All times on this page are GMT

PREDICTIONS

The Full Moon on 4 December falls in the tenth house at London. Mercury is opposed to Uranus and in a harmonious trine with Saturn and Neptune. The government is in a strong position but there will be successful legal challenges to central planks of its programme. We will see major technological advances and new inventions hit the marketplace. Russia is at a significant turning point in its history and there is a chance that some republics may attempt to break away, sparking internal conflict. The USA is also in a period of democratic volatility, with individual states defying the federal government.

The New Moon on 20 December falls in Sagittarius in an exact conjunction with Mercury and a square to Saturn and Neptune. There is an intense focus on religious, philosophical and ideological goals and a neglect of practicalities. Confusion will affect the Church, health service, the employment market and transport and aviation. There may be significant developments in space travel, with plans for a Moon colony now firmly on the international agenda. India could be taking the lead in this area, seeking to become a space super-power, competing with the USA.

The *King George VI Chase* at Kempton may see a 7-year-old outsider win. The Welsh *Grand National* at Chepstow may go to a 6-year-old carrying 10st 2lb.

Old Moore calculates your own birth chart

Your very own personal horoscope by **Old Moore**

The timeless wisdom of **Old Moore** *can now be interpreted by computer – to give you an astounding wealth of insights and revelations.*

At last, the huge analytical power of the computer has been harnessed to the legendary forecasting skills of **Old Moore**.

By revealing the mysteries held within your own astrological chart, you will gain a unique insight into yourself and find a new path to your future which you yourself can influence.

It is based on the **Old Moore** prediction system, which has proved to be uniquely successful and accurate for over three hundred years.

Now it focuses entirely on *YOU*. The result is your very own *character profile and forecast horoscope* for the next twelve months.

Send off the coupon below with your remittance of £20.00, and enjoy a unique view of your future.

12-month Horoscope Book – personal to you – for only £20.00 INCLUDING P&P.

* **Most detailed astral reading of its kind.**
* **CHARACTER PROFILE explores the depths of your true self.**
* **PERSONAL FORECAST predicts ways to improve your happiness and success.**
* **In a tradition of accurate forecasting since 1697.**

YOUR DATE WITH DESTINY...

UNIQUE GIFT IDEA – SEND THIS COUPON NOW!

*Your **Old Moore Personal Horoscope** costs just £20.00 (Please allow 28 days for delivery)*

Name ....
Address ....
....
Postcode ....
Telephone ....
Email ....
Date and year of birth ....
Time of birth (if known) ....
Place of birth ....

Use your credit card to order online at www.foulsham.com and enter your date, time and place of birth on the order form.

Or send this completed form to
W. Foulsham & Co. Ltd, Personal Horoscopes, The Old Barrel Store, Drayman's Lane, Marlow, Bucks SL7 2FF.

Please print clearly in BLOCK CAPITALS.

Make cheques payable to W. Foulsham & Co. Ltd.

If you prefer not to receive mailings from companies other than those connected to Old Moore, please tick the box ☐

Catherine, Princess of Wales

© Doug Peters/Alamy Live News

According to a recent poll, Catherine, HRH The Princess of Wales, is Britain's favourite member of the royal family. Catherine's popularity is long-standing and certainly predates any sympathy generated by her present unfortunate health difficulties. It's not hard to see why this is the case because Kate, as she is known by almost everyone, is a caring, listening and until recently, very busy member of the Royal Family, who in terms of personality could have been made for the job she has occupied since she married Prince William in 2011. Such is her warmth that millions of people feel they know her and make it clear that they like what they know.

Kate was born on 9 January 1982 and it is undoubtedly the position of her Moon in its own home of Cancer that gives her the gentle sensitivity that we see in her public engagements, and which will extend to members of her own family. This powerful planetary influence helps her constantly, especially in the support she offers to mental health charities, and in this and her other extensive charitable work the Cancer Moon is aided by a strong work ethic supplied by the Sun in Capricorn and communicative Mercury in Aquarius. In a holistic sense Kate's astrological chart offers her a range of planetary positions and associations that allow her to understand and to open up to others in a way that is quite unique, and which would have been a part of her nature no matter what her position in life had turned out to be.

What Kate is perhaps slightly less good at is being gentle on herself. Her Capricorn Sun in opposition to her Moon in Cancer is almost certain to bring great frustration and personal distress regarding her own recent health difficulties. She may struggle if she feels she is not making the immediate progress she would wish. She must learn to be patient with herself and focus on her road to recovery.

The Princess of Wales is desperately missed by the publlc at this time. She is admired and respected in Britain and across the world and she is a beacon when it comes to demonstrating what the best of Royals should be. For the moment we can only offer her our best wishes. If Kate possesses one sterling quality that will help her through the difficult times she has been experiencing recently, that quality is a dogged Capricorn determination. This combined with the love and good wishes of millions will help to speed her towards brighter times. It is fortunate that in addition to those qualities that make her so indispensible to the Royals, as well as to her family, Kate carries the qualities of a quiet but determined fighter, together with good, Earth sign resilience.

Will Emma go from Woman's Hour to stardom?

Emma Barnett

© Piers Allardyce/Shutterstock

Emma Barnett is a broadcaster and journalist who has frequently appeared on our radios and television screens and has also written for several newspapers and magazines. She became particularly well known for presenting the BBC's *Woman's Hour*, which she left in 2024 to move to the prestigious *Today* programme. Emma was born on 5 February 1985 and her astrological chart shows her to be intelligent, shrewd and adaptable. Although we do not have her time of birth it is obvious from her Aquarian Sun, Mars in dominant Aries and Mercury alongside the Sun in Aquarius that she is a good and confident speaker, whilst the general balance of her astrological chart is such that she would have found success, no matter what career path she had chosen.

Some planetary squares and the position of Venus in Aries account for the difficult situations associated with Emma's father and brother that might have been a blockage to her own progress in life had she been less of a dynamic personality than she is, but it seems as though she was able to put these family problems to one side and forge ahead in spite of them. After gaining a degree in history and politics at Nottingham University she began her career working for LBC and then went on to work for BBC's Radio Five Live. After this she wrote for several newspapers and eventually won the plum spot presenting *Woman's Hour*, for which she gained not only significant praise but also established herself as a recognisable name.

The sign of Aquarius is strong in Emma's birth chart. This makes her original but also adaptable and she is a communicator *par excellence*. She knows instinctively when to allow the natural edge in her personality to show but senses those occasions when silence tells a better story than too many words. She is incisive but never strays into controversy, remains popular with her listeners and readers and displays her natural versatility in everything she undertakes.

Emma Barnett has been married since 2012 and has a son and a daughter. The demands of family life probably crowd in on her at times because hers is a very busy astrological chart and the twists and turns of her career path show that she must keep many balls in the air when dealing with the various facets of her life. Her chart demonstrates that she will need to pay particular attention to health issues in the years ahead and so much Aquarius in her chart might make that difficult. She could be headed for a major television offer within the next year, which might make her more of a household name.

Emma Barnett's chart bears all the astrological hallmarks of continued success and a personal balance that will always stand her in good stead.

Libra: how to make the most of 2025

LIBRA BORN PEOPLE
Birthdays: 24 September to 23 October inclusive
Planet: Venus. Birthstone: Opal. Lucky day: Friday

Keynote for the Year: *Work may seem quite a chore until the midpoint of the year when new career opportunities are something to watch for – these could be life enhancing.*

JANUARY: MAIN TRENDS: 2–4 Trends highlight your personal money. Use your energy and resourcefulness to firm up your finances and long-term budgets. **15–16** You have a talent for communication and a good memory, but you're also probably easily bored and not keen on routine. **20–21** A turning point in personal or professional affairs when your power to effect positive change is greater than you imagine. **KEY DATES: HIGHS 19–21** Make an early start on important activities when your energy is at its highpoint. **LOWS 6–7** Prepare to contend with some limitations and avoid being over ambitious.

FEBRUARY: MAIN TRENDS: 1–2 A new planetary influence will remind you that life isn't all about work; this should be an enlivening period for your personal life, when partners and friends enrich your life. **7–8** Travel occupies your thoughts but if it's not possible, mixing with a variety of people should keep you happy. **19–20** Curiosity is no bad thing, and you may develop new and exciting ideas – but don't rush a decision over a current project. **KEY DATES: HIGHS 15–17** A very favourable trend that helps you achieve your goals. **LOWS 3–4** Any high hopes for a recent ambition may fail to come off; but at least you can move on now.

MARCH: MAIN TRENDS: 6–7 Professional relationships are now supportive and reassuring, and career success is aided by that same sense of knowing the right people. **12–13** Trends move on, and now you get most from domestic life and the home – let significant others know how much you care about them. **20–21** With improved vitality and ideas for the future, make a fresh start but remember that research can pay real long-term dividends. **KEY DATES: HIGHS 15–16** Heed your intuition now. Benefits may come through people in authority. **LOWS 1–2; 29–30** Deal with a problem from the past, the sooner the better.

APRIL: MAIN TRENDS: 1–2 A good time to analyse yourself and your relationships. There may be minor difficulties in your personal life which require patience. **16–17** You won't have much time to be bored as interesting ideas and people come your way – there may be more social invitations you really have time for! **21–22** If you're working as part of a group, it should be supportive and friendly, and you should get the best from it. **KEY DATES: HIGHS 11–13** Keep your eyes and ears open for new information related to current endeavours. **LOWS 25–26** The lunar low hampers your efforts in all areas but this trend will pass.

MAY: MAIN TRENDS: 4–5 Trends continue to indicate positive change for your social life. Also, in a creative mood you will enjoy the more leisurely side of life. **12–13** Be willing to readjust life goals according to the outcome of this testing period. The truly valid elements of life will survive; let go of the rest. **21–22** Charisma is your middle name now as you find yourself in the best, most interesting, of company. **KEY DATES: HIGHS 8–10** You won't shy away from burning the candle at both ends but this may have varying degrees of success. **LOWS 23–24** There may be minor mishaps behind the scenes. Keep a low profile and rest.

JUNE: MAIN TRENDS: 8–9 You reach another peak in your career as you improve your lines of communication can see the way ahead clearly. **13–15** Personal relationships boost your ego now. Your partner may even let you get away with anything! **22–23** Though you benefit from having plenty of interests on the go, beware of scattering your energy through lack of focus and other distractions.

Libra: maximise your potential every month

KEY DATES: HIGHS 5–6 You are very sharp mentally – make the most of this by exploring new ideas and new ways of thinking. **LOWS 19–20** Keep your own counsel – you may find that your opinions are not well received.

JULY: MAIN TRENDS: 7–8 Expect to make good progress on home improvement projects. With trends favouring domesticity, your family relations should improve with sensitivity and a little initiative on your part. **10–11** An uplift at work should see you with all the help you need in the short term. **22–23** You'll want to get on with things at work but beware, this is not the time to be frustrated with a slow-moving world. **KEY DATES: HIGHS 2–3; 29–31** In an optimistic mood, you should fulfil your expectations, especially if you use your superior judgment. **LOWS 16–17** Take care if you must make a major decision as you lack focus and are a little absent minded.

AUGUST: MAIN TRENDS: 1–2 A diverse range of tasks and jobs may be materially fulfilling and successful. Your curiosity on a certain topic may be more than satisfied. **6–7** Your imagination may be working overtime so keep your feet on the ground and don't let anyone pull the wool over your eyes. **23–24** Making new acquaintances can be quite exciting now and there is much to discuss. Be bold in your approach. **KEY DATES: HIGHS 26–27** Remember that faith can move mountains, and positive thinking can bring great benefits. **LOWS 12–14** Progress will be slow and action difficult. Patience will help this phase pass.

SEPTEMBER: MAIN TRENDS: 1–3 Very much the pioneer with Mars now in your sign, seize any new opportunities but don't assume your work methods are better than anyone else's. **15–16** A hard working period, not without rewards, but beware of any kind of impatience around money, whether in business dealings, investments or any financial arena. **24–25** You may feel restless now, bored by routine. Counter this by getting out or seeking something educational. **KEY DATES: HIGHS 22–23** This influence brings renewed optimism and self-confidence as others are likely to trust in you. **LOWS 9–10** Accept the limitaions of the low and avoid any impetuousness.

OCTOBER: MAIN TRENDS: 8–9 A positive period for personal relationships and an excellent time for joint/co-operative ventures, whether pleasure or business. **14–15** Express your ideas fluently and you should see them come to fruition. **24–25** Trends increase your attractiveness and personal warmth so expect people to reach out to you. An almost perfect time to start a brand-new relationship. **KEY DATES: HIGHS 19–21** The lunar high may bring you the knack of persuading a superior to be of considerable help. **LOWS 6–7** A less than lucky time so avoid beginning anything new and instead focus on recharging your batteries.

NOVEMBER: MAIN TRENDS: 5–6 Put some constructive energy and action into communication: writing, reading and anything intellectual. Get all your little tasks finished. **12–13** An excellent time to take care of business – you may not be free to do as you wish but can accomplish much if you stay focused. **22–23** Be ruthless now when it comes to making personal changes if you can see a clear path towards the future. **KEY DATES: HIGHS 15–17** You know that with hard work you can accomplish a great deal professionally. A promotion or new job may arise now. **LOWS 3–4; 30** A problematic period. Avoid any tense situations and focus on rest and relaxation if you can.

DECEMBER: MAIN TRENDS: 3–4 With your attractiveness at a peak, there may be new romantic beginnings for some Librans, or a period of domestic harmony for those in relationships. **18–19** Emotions may be unstable, so focus instead on your work commitments. Discipline your energy towards realistic goals. **22–23** Someone at home may be stressed over a personal matter; you may feel their reaction is exaggerated, but handle this carefully. Try to see the wider picture. **KEY DATES: HIGHS 13–14** Make the most of this go-ahead phase – you have boundless energy and the planets behind you. **LOWS 1; 27–28** You may lack perspective so refrain from making important decisions until this influence has passed.

Scorpio: what's ahead in 2025?

SCORPIO BORN PEOPLE
Birthdays: 24 October to 22 November inclusive
Planets: Mars, Pluto. Birthstone: Topaz. Lucky day: Tuesday

Keynote for the Year: *A year which may see growth and opportunity in joint financial matters, although a romantic issue may well have you thinking twice.*

JANUARY: MAIN TRENDS: 5–6 Avoid making decisions on impulse right now; trends suggest you may be being led in the wrong direction or deceived, by others or even yourself. **14–16** Your best area of life is now your home and family. Anything nostalgic should also appeal to you. **20–21** Try to accommodate the needs of others in your push for better organisation and progress – and don't over-dramatise problems at work. **KEY DATES: HIGHS 22–23** In high spirits and with boundless energy, you can get away with just about anything. Put your luck to the test. **LOWS 8–9** A quiet time – put any grandiose schemes on the back burner.

FEBRUARY: MAIN TRENDS: 11–12 Trends suggest that a new and unforeseen opportunity to meet people and make friends may arise. This is also a good time to consolidate existing friendships. **13–14** It may be necessary to strike a balance between fulfilling your own needs and your obligations to others. Remember this during this particular Valentine's Day! **19–20** You should have plenty of opportunity to let your light shine and impress others in social encounters. **KEY DATES: HIGHS 18–19** Take any opportunity to direct events at work; you should find it easy to enlist the support of colleagues. **LOWS 4–5** Beware of free advice – there may be some deceptive influences about.

MARCH: MAIN TRENDS: 7–8 You're at your best trying to find original ideas and during the search, you may learn something new about yourself. **10–11** Your personality is sparkling, so perhaps you can use it to persuade others to follow your lead, especially in ambitious matters. **20–21** Your plans should meet little resistance, though you're more concerned with efficiency than personal recognition. **KEY DATES: HIGHS 17–19** The green light for go is on and this should spell faster progress. **LOWS 3–5; 31** Although slightly pessimistic, you are sensitive towards others. Just take care not to exhaust yourself.

APRIL: MAIN TRENDS: 2–3 Press ahead to give yourself the advantage – right now there may be more than just one, Scorpio. **4–5** This is a great time for professional planning; you work diligently and items on your agenda see you building up strength and security for the future. **21–22** You have good leadership skills, but it is vital that you assert yourself in a positive and non-confrontational manner. **KEY DATES: HIGHS 14–15** Your judgement is good and problem solving is as easy as ABC during this lunar high. **LOWS 1; 29–30** You may struggle to keep up the pace of progress; beware of biting off more than you can chew.

MAY: MAIN TRENDS: 5–6 Money matters and practical affairs may prove an area of growth, and there may be news now regarding new monetary opportunities. **17–18** Think hard about jettisoning something from your life. It's time to get rid of any dead wood and get to the nub of personal problems. **21–22** Social contacts seem to fall nicely into place. Go out of your way to help others now and just see how rewarding this can be. **KEY DATES: HIGHS 11–12** A personal boost. You are quick to grasp new ideas and prone to flashes of insight. **LOWS 25–26** Put new ideas to one side for a while and slow down the pace.

JUNE: MAIN TRENDS: 5–6 At work things seem to be moving along quite smoothly with plenty of productive results to show for it. **14–15** A supportive influence in more ways than one: the planets are behind you on financial projects now, and help you find emotional support from your partner. **23–24** Though practical aims seem to be on target, beware any tendency to impatience with limitations.

Scorpio: pinpoint the best days for you

Delegate tasks to others if necessary. **KEY DATES: HIGHS 7–9** Your highly original way of dealing with life's issues may lead to a breakthrough. **LOWS 21–22** You may be confronted with large amounts of work. Take a simple approach and tackle it methodically.

JULY: MAIN TRENDS: 1–2 Keep up a varied and interesting social life and look forward to some happy encounters where you may learn something significant. **15–16** Life may seem a chore right now, even with plenty of self-determination. Remember that this phase will pass. **23–24** Personal relationships may now bring some of the best information your way; there is much of interest going on socially and this can impact positively on other areas. **KEY DATES: HIGHS 4–6** Push your luck just a little and consider taking a small, measured chance. **LOWS 18–19** Relax and take things easy, as your energy will deplete too easily now.

AUGUST: MAIN TRENDS: 2–3 Keep up your own momentum and don't allow the views of others to influence your actions in any significant way. Make your own mind up. **11–12** Life for you is now all enjoyment, leisure and romance. Enjoy it – and use your abundant creative energy. **23–24** You are highly sensitive to your environment and to other people. This can work wonders in any discussions or negotiations. **KEY DATES: HIGHS 28–30** Look out for any new opportunity, whether personal or career based – who knows to where it'll lead? **LOWS 15–16** Take a back seat in a practical matter during this temporary lull.

SEPTEMBER: MAIN TRENDS: 5–6 Express your opinion clearly during any discussion with your partner. Secrets and lack of clarity can lead to mishaps. **16–17** Right now you may have a good instinct for teamwork. You have the knack of dealing with other people on their own level and keeping them on side. **27–28** Certain duties may test your patience now, but only because of disorganisation – try to stay on top! **KEY DATES: HIGHS 24–26** A good time to make progress in the realisation of dreams and schemes. **LOWS 11–12** Indulge your instinct to shut out the world for a while, if you can.

OCTOBER: MAIN TRENDS: 13–14 You may be inspired by the wide horizon, and this may lead to travel for fun and pleasure. Absorb as much culture as you can. **15–16** A period of potential financial advancement, which may be assisted by a loved one in some way. Practical matters also improve through the kindly help of colleagues and friends. **24–25** Consider removing any deadwood and obstructions from your life – you can spot potential problems a mile away. **KEY DATES: HIGHS 22–23** Positive thinking reaps positive rewards under the lunar high. **LOWS 8–9** Find the right work–life balance: meet your obligations, then think of yourself.

NOVEMBER: MAIN TRENDS: 8–9 Trends favour social gatherings, especially in large groups. Your talent is for putting others at their ease. **10–11** A theme of renewal pervades, as you can clearly see which elements of life are worth keeping and where you should move on. **22–23** A trip down memory lane should be enjoyable, but any domestic situation is favoured now. **KEY DATES: HIGHS 18–19** You may achieve something of significance during these positive days and it may seem that no matter what you do, you can't fail. **LOWS 5–6** Prepare for some career difficulties and delays, possibly because of low energy.

DECEMBER: MAIN TRENDS: 6–7 A very favourable period for group events – the more the merrier far as you are concerned. You may get a chance to make new associates along the way. **9–10** You do well to avoid confrontation at this time – but there's a danger that this may lead you to underestimate issues when, in fact, there are problems to be faced. **22–23** You look and feel strong in pursuit of your objectives – just don't allow yourself to become overconfident. **KEY DATES: HIGHS 15–17** You're more ambitious than usual and you have the self-confidence to take on big tasks. Make the most of it. **LOWS 2–3; 29–31** A time when your powers may be rather ineffectual, so keep a low profile and focus on personal matters.

SAGITTARIUS BORN PEOPLE
Birthdays: 23 November to 21 December inclusive
Planet: Jupiter. Birthstone: Turquoise. Lucky day: Thursday

Keynote for the Year: *Domestic matters may bring new responsibilities to work through, though personal and emotional relationships are a growth area for much of the year.*

JANUARY: MAIN TRENDS: 5–6 If you take things for granted at home, you may find it backfires on you. Play it cool and stay on the right side of loved ones. **16–17** You have more patience than usual and can work more efficiently – professional relationships are a source of mutual benefit. **20–21** A good time for a break or just plain having fun. You are inclined to feel lazy, and time spent with your partner could be appealing. **KEY DATES: HIGHS 24–26** The emphasis is on communication – focus on connecting with others and keeping informed. **LOWS 10–11** Troubled by self-doubt and delays, step back and accept what you cannot control.

FEBRUARY: MAIN TRENDS: 8–9 Don't allow others to dominate what you say or do – trust your instincts in important personal matters. **13–14** A breezy period when you will enjoy meeting new stimulating people and getting out and about. **19–20** This influence should have a pleasant effect on social matters – a good time to enjoy and consolidate existing friendships. Perhaps arrange a social occasion? **KEY DATES: HIGHS 22–23** News learnt in the workplace could now unearth some vital information. Be alert to what's happening around you. **LOWS 6–7** Heavy responsibilities may frustrate you and vitality is low, so go easy.

MARCH: MAIN TRENDS: 3–4 Co-operate with others, especially socially. Information received now may lead to personal achievement. **12–13** With good powers of concentration, now's the time to make a decision about a business relationship or financial deal. **22–23** You need to feel useful, and could be enjoying fixing or improving things, whether at home or at work. **KEY DATES: HIGHS 20–21** What you hear from others may helpfully contribute to current objectives. Try to avoid busy schedules and heavy demands. **LOWS 6–7** There may be something holding you back, and during this period you may lack the energy to overcome it. This trend is temporary.

APRIL: MAIN TRENDS: 4–5 Happy social encounters tend to coincide with this influence, and you should be bringing out the best in everyone you meet. **6–7** The pace of life may quicken as you have less time to fulfil your agenda – make sure you don't overreach yourself. **21–22** Efficient at work, your thinking tends to be both creative and practical, and the results are worth having. **KEY DATES: HIGHS 16–18** Trends continue to bring you positive influence over your colleagues at work and enhance your persuasive skills too! **LOWS 2–3; 29–30** Slow down the action and pace yourself now.

MAY: MAIN TRENDS: 9–10 Loved ones make life rewarding; you needn't worry about feeling alone with so much emotional support. **20–21** You may be asked to adjust your ambitions; your energy levels may also be low but don't use any of this as an excuse for not doing your best. **22–23** You may feel that life is really going somewhere now. Tremendous results are to be had by maintaining a wide social circle. **KEY DATES: HIGHS 13–15** This can be a phase of expanding opportunity and, perhaps, financial benefits. **LOWS 27–28** You may be solving far more problems than usual, but you will need to think carefully about your next move.

JUNE: MAIN TRENDS: 5–6 You have ingenious and original ideas. New and exciting opportunities may come about through a conversation. **7–8** You benefit from freedom of movement – this is not a day to be stuck with mundane routine. Enjoy what the social world has to offer, if possible. **25–26** Professional interests are highlighted – new projects are likely, and you will also improve your communication skills

Sagittarius: a guide to your good-luck days

at work. **KEY DATES: HIGHS 10–11** You may now have the chance to gain more control of your own destiny – use your intuition to aim for worthwhile, productive goals. **LOWS 23–24** It may be a case of one step forward, two steps back; take it easy and let the rest of the world go by.

JULY: MAIN TRENDS: 4–5 Your vitality and charm can now make you popular with everyone. It's the perfect time for social activities or just gathering new information – useful or otherwise! **12–13** You may need to spend some time by yourself for long periods; this may help to put certain matters in perspective. **23–24** This enhances your sense of enterprise and initiative, though sacrifices will have to be made to preserve the status quo at home. **KEY DATES: HIGHS 7–8** Traditionally, a time when things get easier. Prepare to make rather a powerful impact on someone. **LOWS 20–22** Go easy on yourself while this influence prevails – for a start, reduce any stress levels in your life.

AUGUST: MAIN TRENDS: 9–10 Events may now bring deeper issues to the fore that must be resolved, and every decision may seem crucial and life changing. Focus on what it is you really want. **14–15** Assume more responsibility at work to help you get ahead fast, but take care if an unexpected, snap decision is called for. **23–24** A phase when things may vanish from your life – how this happens depends on whether you are willing to voluntarily make serious changes, especially in relationships. **KEY DATES: HIGHS 3–4; 31** Confidence and zeal are your support in a practical matter. **LOWS 17–18** Focus on your priorities and don't be swayed by the expectations of others.

SEPTEMBER: MAIN TRENDS: 2–3 Now is the time to broaden your horizons whether physically or mentally. Dwell on new philosophies or take a trip somewhere. **6–7** Your mind is quick and alert and your curiosity may be aroused by new ideas or information. **23–24** Once again, any travel is beneficial so get out and about as much as you can and stimulate the little grey cells. **KEY DATES: HIGHS 1; 27–28** The lunar high aids your persuasiveness and might even mean that a boss or superior comes around to your way of thinking. **LOWS 13–14** Beware – too much worry could create the very problems that you are trying to avoid.

OCTOBER: MAIN TRENDS: 1–2 Take any opportunity to get outside and enjoy the outdoor life. Also, continue to be open to new ideas. **15–16** Romantic relationships should be going well, but you are at your best with anyone who you find stimulating and fun. Others may find you entertaining company. **27–28** Expect emotional and domestic tranquillity, and emotional support when you need it. Property matters should go well. **KEY DATES: HIGHS 24–26** Don't dither or hold back if you want to make a personal connection. **LOWS 10–11** Trends indicate a delay to communication – you may find yourself endlessly waiting for information.

NOVEMBER: MAIN TRENDS: 1–3 If you can avoid mundane routine so much the better; the need to explore is strong and you benefit from the weird and wonderful. **4–5** You will enjoy being part of the team now; you can learn from others in the group and there may be new acquaintances on the horizon. **23–24** This trend invigorates most relationships, but if you're currently single, you may meet a new love interest under this influence. **KEY DATES: HIGHS 20–22** Take control and make any necessary changes to major plans. **LOWS 7–8** It's now obvious that very little of importance will get done – it's simply the wrong time to act.

DECEMBER: MAIN TRENDS: 1–3 Trends place a powerful emphasis on personal security and point to satisfying results. You may even make a small monetary gain. **8–9** Keep apart from the crowd and display your unique identity. Others may find this influential. **21–22** You are sensitive to the feelings of those around you and may offer good counsel. Take time for yourself, too. **KEY DATES: HIGHS 18–19** Projects may conclude satisfactorily or, equally, brand new ones may get off the ground. **LOWS 4–5** You may be better off working alone and sticking to practical matters.

CAPRICORN BORN PEOPLE
Birthdays: 22 December to 20 January inclusive
Planet: Saturn. Birthstone: Garnet. Lucky day: Saturday

Keynote for the Year: *Work performance and productivity can be high early this year but the tone changes by July when your real growth area is personal relationships.*

JANUARY: MAIN TRENDS: 2–3 Income and resources are highlighted so review your budget and savings; you may have the opportunity to bolster your economic outlook. **14–15** You are very communicative, not a little curious, and like to talk now. Learning and fact finding of all kinds may be of practical benefit. **KEY DATES: HIGHS 27–28** With good energy levels, you may have an uncanny knack of succeeding with certain major initiatives. **LOWS 12–13** A brief sense of failure may prompt you to reassess long-term goals. Don't make any rash decisions and remember you are under the effect of the lunar low.

FEBRUARY: MAIN TRENDS: 2–3 Your mind is pretty sharp, but others won't appreciate your opinions if you make them forcefully or impatiently. **11–12** Don't take on too many practical commitments now – you're unlikely to complete them all. Take one thing at a time. **19–20** A great time to be part of a team or among groups; be on the lookout for social newcomers who could soon prove valuable in one way or another. **KEY DATES: HIGHS 23–24** Enthusiasm and self-confidence are running high, and there's very little that will get you down. **LOWS 8–10** Try to keep life simple and undemanding, as much as is possible anyway.

MARCH: MAIN TRENDS: 10–11 The focus is on relationships, and partnerships could bring rewards. A phase when honest, straight-forward discussions will dispel worries and simplify life. **14–15** Trends influence problem solving, and this will come from sound intuition and taking the right action. A time for 'off with the old and on with the new'. **20–21** Expect some changes in your personal life and go with the flow. This gives you the opportunity to do things differently and make fresh starts. **KEY DATES: HIGHS 22–24** Have faith in yourself and you will create the optimal conditions for success! **LOWS 8–9** Prepare to face some challenging situations now. Ride out the trend.

APRIL: MAIN TRENDS: 6–7 Overcome difficulties in your life by directly confronting them, making responsible issues out of them, and by challenging them. **11–12** In high spirits and with the emphasis on leisure, get out and do your own thing; others may join you. **21–22** Things may seem far more urgent than they really are, so pace yourself. Avoid unnecessary run ins with others by burning off any excess energy. **KEY DATES: HIGHS 19–20** High energy levels should enable you to tackle demanding work or, perhaps, sporting activities. **LOWS 4–5** Don't believe everything you hear now or be in such a hurry to get ahead.

MAY: MAIN TRENDS: 4–5 Expect some relationship pressures now and to get too little of your own way! Patience and understanding are required if good things are to develop. **14–15** A nostalgic mood seems apparent and journeys down memory lane should prove rewarding; go on, indulge yourself in the past. **22–23** Trends favour communication – meeting people and creating contacts are a way to keep yourself up-to-date on all the latest developments. **KEY DATES: HIGHS 16–17** As self-confidence is running high, things tend to get done – successfully too! **LOWS 1–2; 29–30** Postpone important personal and business decisions during the lunar low.

JUNE: MAIN TRENDS: 1–2 In business matters be careful and reflective, and always lean towards safety, rather than risk to get the best from your working life. **3–4** Your optimistic outlook will lift you and bring out the best in others. A short journey might prove utterly rewarding. **22–23** Break out of

Capricorn: plan ahead to make the most of your luck

mundane routine and explore the outdoor world to expand your horizons. **KEY DATES: HIGHS 12–13** There is potential for growth, and your willingness to gather new experiences can mean positive change. **LOWS 25–26** Self-doubt could create problems where there were none in the first place. Recognise that this is simply tiredness.

JULY: MAIN TRENDS: 13–14 You may have private goals to be realised now as domestic life takes centre stage. If you need to ignore the outside world for a while, so be it. **20–21** Seize the limelight and let others know just who you are. Someone new may put their trust in you. **25–26** A favourable time for business communications and investments when long-term plans can be clarified, and thinking is realistic. **KEY DATES: HIGHS 9–11** Focus your energy on work and your career – trends suggest that a 'once in a lifetime' opportunity may now come your way! **LOWS 23–24** Avoid potential pitfalls by winding down certain activities.

AUGUST: MAIN TRENDS: 1–2 A hectic phase of events may lie ahead but you seem to be getting things together nicely. **8–9** Trust your intuition, it won't let you down, but keep the scope of your plans realistic. **23–24** Don't be afraid to head out and seek the wide blue yonder. You may enjoy and benefit from travel because of the opportunities it gives you to learn. **KEY DATES: HIGHS 6–7** Be prepared to put body and soul into everything you do and it will not go unnoticed. **LOWS 19–20** You may find your progress at work is much slacker – keep major plans up your sleeve until the low has passed.

SEPTEMBER: MAIN TRENDS: 6–7 Planetary influences help you relate to others, especially on a personal level. Look out for any opportunity for gain. **17–18** Don't let this become a downward trend when dreams and schemes fall flat – reduce some of your considerable expectations and things should work out. **23–24** Plan your workload carefully to get through your responsibilities. Certain material plans ought to be doing rather nicely. **KEY DATES: HIGHS 2–3; 29–30** Confidence and charm are in ready supply, and you make a big impact on others. **LOWS 15–16** Slow things down and prepare for a few inevitable minor setbacks.

OCTOBER: MAIN TRENDS: 2–3 Clear life's deadwood and the path to growth and progress will become clear. New ideas are essential as is putting them into practice. **18–19** Charm gets you what you want at this stage, so make the most of it. Romance of the soul-stirring kind would seem a real possibility. **23–24** This period is all about personal growth, especially in your career. Try to organise a meeting or discussion with someone who could help you progress. **KEY DATES: HIGHS 27–28** You have an air of self-confidence now – use it to expand and set new plans into action. **LOWS 12–13** The low leaves you feeling held back; ride out the trend.

NOVEMBER: MAIN TRENDS: 7–8 You'll be on a roll at work with loads of energy to spare. Projects in which you can work independently are best favoured. **15–16** A time of creativity and good things in your love life when grabbing the spotlight and stealing the scene gives you a thrill. **22–23** The pace of life quickens and you may struggle to concentrate on one thing at a time. Keep focused before events overtake you. **KEY DATES: HIGHS 23–24** An innovative mood takes over and big changes may be on the way in a professional environment. **LOWS 9–10** Expect to have to contend with delays – cut your losses and move on.

DECEMBER: MAIN TRENDS: 1–2 Working with others could be enjoyable and most business negotiations should go well – there may be an unexpected boost. **10–11** A beneficial phase in relationships, and social matters are also apt to be enhanced. Time to shower feelings of warmth and affection on everyone around you. **23–24** In career matters you can throw caution to the winds and plan to go after what you really want – give some thought to your work plans for the year ahead. **KEY DATES: HIGHS 20–22** Broaden your reach and refuse to limit your possibilities, especially in the workplace. **LOWS 6–7** The planets seem to conspire to get you to take things at a slower pace. Take the hint!

Aquarius: your optimum days in 2025

AQUARIUS BORN PEOPLE
Birthdays: 21 January to 19 February inclusive
Planets: Saturn, Uranus. **Birthstone:** Amethyst. **Lucky day:** Saturday

Keynote for the Year: Financially, events are likely to keep your feet on the ground, though by July opportunities in the workplace may become a real possibility.

JANUARY: MAIN TRENDS: 5–6 Professionally, many things may look bright as astrological trends show new projects properly up and running. **11–12** If you feel you know the right steps to take, go ahead and take them; you may go from strength to strength, especially at work. **20–21** This is the right time to make important contacts, so reach out with phone calls, e-mails or even letters. Also, a period when disputes could now be satisfactorily resolved. **KEY DATES: HIGHS 29–30** Get ready to set major plans into motion before you lose the inspiration. **LOWS 14–16** A period of likely low energy when you should pace yourself.

FEBRUARY: MAIN TRENDS: 7–8 You may now receive some unexpected news. Don't be impatient with those who can't keep up with your lightning quick speed. **13–14** If you hit some setbacks financially, accepting the change and developing more flexibility would bring benefits now. **19–20** Hearth and home offer respite from whatever demands are placed on you. A journey into your past puts a smile on your face. **KEY DATES: HIGHS 25–26** A rather lucky trend for general progress, but you'll have to strike while the iron is hot. **LOWS 11–12** Life can be hectic and tiresome at this time – don't allow minor detail to overwhelm you.

MARCH: MAIN TRENDS: A good day for short trips and visits to close friends. Closer to home, your ties to another may bring unexpected rewards. **16–17** Versatility is your strength so you can handle several different interests successfully now. Multi-tasking suits you. **20–21** Not the best day for detailed thinking even though it may be worthwhile considering what's important, and what your next big move will be. **KEY DATES: HIGHS 25–26** Life should be fulfilling, and others supportive of your plans and objectives. **LOWS 10–11** Some delays are inevitable but take a back-up role and let partners handle major decisions.

APRIL: MAIN TRENDS: 2–4 Social invitations may come thick and fast. You may also find that others really want to help you in your endeavours. **9–10** You may not be assertive enough in a certain situation. Although you may not want to take charge, don't let others do this either. **23–24** You should be looking and feeling your best; social and romantic encounters may boost this feeling of self-confidence. **KEY DATES: HIGHS 21–22** You're not afraid to start new projects, take on challenges and advance your practical goals under the lunar high. **LOWS 6–8** If you feel rather uninspired take time out to recharge your batteries.

MAY: MAIN TRENDS: 6–7 Stay on the move and broaden your horizons during this optimistic time. **15–17** Trends assist you to be assertive to good effect, so seek out the spotlight and make your unique mark upon the world. **22–23** Make good use of the positive planetary influences over your finances; set out to accomplish uncompleted tasks and build upon recent beginnings. **KEY DATES: HIGHS 18–19** Take the initiative in your present situation and make changes. Most projects roll along smoothly. **LOWS 3–5** Treat this as a lay off period between one important job and the next. This will save time and energy in the long run.

JUNE: MAIN TRENDS: 4–5 Some personal situations could be rather insecure now, and old ones may even be severed but be positive as new ones will eventually come into being. **12–13** Beware – certain quickly conceived plans and ideas might seem attractive at first glance but they might not look so good later. **22–23** A generally lucky trend but an especially great time for partnerships so get out to meet

Aquarius: tune into your lucky times

friends, old or new. **KEY DATES: HIGHS 14–16** The way is now clear for you to emerge from any setback and move forward – go for it! **LOWS 1; 27–28** You may feel the need to withdraw and do a little soul-searching – give yourself the space to do so.

JULY: MAIN TRENDS: 4–6 Although you may be busy, take time out for a conversation with someone – it may be of surprising benefit to you; you never know what you'll learn. **10–11** Potentially a demanding, tiring and pressurised time at work. Make sure you keep on the right side of superiors. **22–23** Another strong influence over your personal life may bring new people into your life, with only a little effort on your part. **KEY DATES: HIGHS 12–13** Enjoy your personal strength at the lucky time of the month. **LOWS 25–26** You may be left waiting for important news, or matters may go unaccountably wrong. Tread carefully.

AUGUST: MAIN TRENDS: 2–4 A period of growth when you can achieve the success you've worked for. Trends may also bring you some financial clout. **11–13** Communications with friends are enhanced by current trends, making this a great time to be out and about picking up new information. **23–25** Your chart indicates some light at the end of the tunnel; a good time to retreat from everyday routine to search for inspiration. **KEY DATES: HIGHS 8–9** Focus on what you really want and set out to define the direction your life should take. **LOWS 21–22** A good time to reorganise your personal life – don't waste time on trivialities or thankless tasks.

SEPTEMBER: MAIN TRENDS: 1–2 Trends are good for personal relationships, especially partnerships; you may attract someone who will share in your interests. **10–12** An enjoyable and rewarding period socially – collaborate with others and forget personal ambitions for a while. **23–24** You may learn something new and rewarding during this positive phase for communication. Discussions and debates may be fruitful. **KEY DATES: HIGHS 4–6** A very advantageous period is now indicated, when you can expect to pull everything together by the sheer force of your personality. **LOWS 17–19** You may lack energy, so attend to life's simpler tasks and get as much rest as possible.

OCTOBER: MAIN TRENDS: 9–10 Organise some social events, express yourself creatively and you should impress some new admirers. **11–12** Dig deep to uncover the root of an emotional issue, especially one in your relationship that may relate to the past. **23–24** Most things in life, but especially career decisions, must now be backed by practical judgement. Don't take any action simply on impulse. **KEY DATES: HIGHS 2–3; 29–30** Practical and efficient, use these skills to move ahead effectively. **LOWS 14–16** Although you will have to strive quite hard for what you want to achieve, make sure to avoid the frantic approach.

NOVEMBER: MAIN TRENDS: 5–6 Opportunities for significant change may arise at work, although this may not be the kind you had envisioned. **18–19** Your social and personal life receives a boost, which flatters your ego. Just be yourself. **22–23** Open your mind to new ideas, and be prepared not only to consider change, but to inaugurate it. **KEY DATES: HIGHS 25–27** Continue to welcome new ideas – this remains a great time for taking the initiative with new concepts. **LOWS 11–12** You may feel that events are conspiring to work against you, slowing your progress to a halt. Remember, this is just the effect of the lunar low and will pass.

DECEMBER: MAIN TRENDS: 3–4 Working in a group or as part of a team is favourably highlighted now, especially in your social circle. **12–14** Personally, certain situations may have run their course – the challenge is to be rid of what's no longer of value. **21–22** Get to grips with things that hold you back and take control of the forces that may thwart your progress. Just deal with them! **KEY DATES: HIGHS 23–24** You enjoy a good challenge and may want to push your luck a little, but remember that it is Christmas Eve. **LOWS 8–9** Under pressure, you may struggle to find solutions or make the right decisions. Rest and go with the flow.

Pisces: your daily guide to 2025

PISCES BORN PEOPLE
Birthdays: 20 February to 20 March inclusive
Planets: Jupiter, Neptune. Birthstone: Bloodstone. Lucky day: Thursday

Keynote for the Year: *With taskmaster Saturn in Pisces in 2025 you have the chance for a fresh start, but a committed, realistic approach is the only one that will work.*

JANUARY: MAIN TRENDS: 2–3 As the year begins, you can open certain doors towards progress – your spirits are strong and there is little you can't do, whether small or large. **11–12** You may lack energy so try to make life less complex and attend to the simpler facets of life. **20–21** Loved ones not only provide emotional support where needed but can probably assist on the material level with the more tangible resources. **KEY DATES: HIGHS 4–5; 31** Make the most of this physical peak as trends give you a real 'pick-me-up'. **LOWS 17–18** Don't fixate on how to achieve certain ends – relax your mind and you may enjoy sudden insight.

FEBRUARY: MAIN TRENDS: 7–8 Home is your best environment now. Plan a social occasion if others are willing, or perhaps consider some home improvements or decorating. **10–11** Mixing business with pleasure may have a positive impact on your ambitions. Certain results are almost guaranteed. **19–20** An exchange of ideas with a like-minded individual may lead to a broadening of your mental horizons. What you learn now could prove fascinating. **KEY DATES: HIGHS 1; 27–28** Meetings with others should go especially well, even becoming a little PR exercise for yourself! There may be some welcoming new faces on the horizon. **LOWS 13–14** You can't always duck problems – sometimes you need to act.

MARCH: MAIN TRENDS: 3–5 Trends bring a boost to money and finances – with the right careful moves you may benefit, but always take professional advice first. **6–7** Energetic and self-assured, there's every reason to think practical matters will go your way. **20–21** A very positive influence should help you eliminate past limitations and replace them with new personal freedom. **KEY DATES: HIGHS 27–28** Continuing very favourable trends may lead to tremendous achievements even, perhaps, successfully reaching a personal ambition. **LOWS 12–14** There are many demands on you currently, so pace yourself.

APRIL: MAIN TRENDS: 13–14 Practical limitations may prove tiresome, and you'll benefit from having something new and interesting to do. Of course, a change is as good as a rest. **15–16** Being more meticulous and attentive than usual, you will feel that if a job's worth doing, it's worth doing very well indeed. **21–22** Freedom is crucial to you; keep your sights broad and be ready and open for anything new. You may be surprised. **KEY DATES: HIGHS 23–24** In a confident mood, this is an excellent day for meetings. **LOWS 9–10** Not the best period for trying to set the world to rights – take time to recuperate instead.

MAY: MAIN TRENDS: 2–3 With a talent for making people welcome, entertaining at home gives you real pleasure now. **14–15** Everything is now geared towards happy social encounters; think only the best of others and they will think the best of you. **23–24** Your sparkling personality sees you on a high and your powers of attraction are strong. A little will power goes a very long way! **KEY DATES: HIGHS 21–22** Whether at work or at home and you can now capitalise on your recent efforts to get ahead. **LOWS 6–7** Focus on one priority; don't overdo things by trying to handle several different matters at once.

JUNE: MAIN TRENDS: 3–4 A high-energy phase when opportunities for advancement in your career are there if you look hard enough. Now is the time to use your persuasive powers. **7–8** If you ring in the changes, you may attract the right sort of people at the right time. The support you need is right there. **22–23** Rewarding influences now surround family and home. Perhaps invite friends over or

Pisces: a guide to your good-luck days

enjoy a trip down memory lane with relatives. **KEY DATES: HIGHS 17–18** Make the most of positive trends influencing your work. **LOWS 2–3** Beware – the lunar low may affect your ability to keep life on an even keel.

JULY: MAIN TRENDS: 9–10 Exciting social plans should now be on your agenda as you take a more freewheeling approach to the affairs of the day. Good things are happening in your personal life. **16–17** Renewal and regeneration are your watchwords, but this may mean dealing with the passing of something that has been important in your life. **22–23** A favourable influence affecting relationships – you do best in situations which make use of your social skills, especially those requiring diplomacy. **KEY DATES: HIGHS 14–15** You should be looking and feeling your stylish best. Put this to some good use! **LOWS 1; 27–28** Be prepared to have to make a serious compromise.

AUGUST: MAIN TRENDS: 1–3 Trends will help you get what you want if you take care to say the right things. **6–7** The forces of change are in place, but you may be trying to hang on to something that isn't working. A fresh start in the most unlikely area may prove a good thing. **26–27** Examine your life to decide what's working and what's not – and why. You may learn a great deal from others. **KEY DATES: HIGHS 10–11** Someone may offer you a special opportunity – follow your curiosity and see where it leads. **LOWS 23–25** If you've made poor decisions, prepare for the fact that you may now learn exactly how poor they were!

SEPTEMBER: MAIN TRENDS: 11–12 Creative activities are favoured, and you're probably quite expressive and sociable now – this makes you popular with others. **13–15** A good phase to be out and about: new opportunities to please yourself and do your own thing (especially travel) should arise. **22–23** Current influences may offer solutions to practical problems, though you should realise that proceeding cautiously is the best way forward. **KEY DATES: HIGHS 7–8** Practical matters receive a helping hand. **LOWS 20–21** Setbacks may be unavoidable and decisions not yours to make – just keep to the tried and tested path.

OCTOBER: MAIN TRENDS: 1–2 Your concern with making money and material progress should receive a boost, though your best area is in the professional sphere. **9–10** Keep your eyes and ears open for useful input and listen to your intuition during this positive phase for communications. **23–24** A period when things go better in your love life. This trend also indicates that winning someone over will boost your ego. **KEY DATES: HIGHS 4–5** Optimistic trends are in operation, so getting big plans up and running may seem easier than usual. **LOWS 17–18** Rest and contemplation is best; don't look for new mountains to climb.

NOVEMBER: MAIN TRENDS: 4–5 Financial matters may prove gratifying – you gain from taking on new challenges that can improve your position in the sphere of money-making. **6–8** You may have to change certain things in your personal life to make improvements to your well-being. Give this some time and thought. **22–23** Professionally, useful contacts may appear and it's not what you know but who you know that helps you get on. **KEY DATES: HIGHS 1–2; 28–29** There's much you can achieve through your positive spirits and efforts under this influence. **LOWS 13–14** A period to just ride with the changes. Find time to recharge your batteries.

DECEMBER: MAIN TRENDS: 1–3 The planets will conspire to bring out your true self. Someone close by should be supporting your goals, while you make a big impact and get what you want. **15–16** Share your emotions and responsibilities with a partner who will take a load off your mind. **21–22** Being rid of deadwood and laying the foundations of future objectives is the order of the day. But go one step at a time. **KEY DATES: HIGHS 25–26** With a little self-determination, getting your own way should be easier than usual this Christmas. Push your luck gently. **LOWS 10–12** Make plenty of time for relaxation and pace yourself – don't expect to get much of your own way.

Back a winner with Old Moore

Racing with the Jockeys in 2025

ASTROLOGICAL POINTERS TO POSSIBLE WINNING PERIODS

The astrologically compiled dates below are presented to race-goers in the hope that they will point the way to some successful winning periods during the 2025 racing season. Specially recommended = sr.

FAVOURABLE PERIODS FOR FLAT-RACE JOCKEYS

O. MURPHY: Born 6 September 1995. To be favoured in weight-for-age races – especially on Midlands courses. His favourable periods are: 8, 15, 19, 25–26 March; 2, 9–10, 19–22, 26–30 April (30 sr); 9, 12–15, 22–24 May (12–15 sr); 10–12, 17–18, 28–29 June (17–18 sr); 1, 10, 18–20, 26–29 July; 1–2, 7, 14–15, 21–25 August; 2–6, 14–17, 26–29 September (2, 29 sr); 8–9, 20, 22–23, 28–31 October; 3, 6–8, 11, 24–29 November (6–8 sr).

H. DOYLE: Born 11 October 1996. Should do well on the longer courses, particularly in the south. Her favourable periods are: 12–18, 21, 24–27, 31 March; 1–2, 4–7, 14–18, 28–30 April; 1–3, 10, 16–18, 30–31 May; 1, 4, 16, 24–27 June (1, 16 sr); 1, 5–9, 14–17, 22, 28–31 July (28–31 sr); 1–3, 15–16, 25 August (1–3, 15–16 sr); 8–9, 11–12, 26–30 September; 2–5, 6–8, 16–18, 22–25 October; 3–7, 15–17, 23–24, 30 November (23–24 sr).

W. BUICK: Born 22 July 1988. Should be a jockey to follow on sprinters especially in late season. His favourable periods are: 22–23, 28–30 March; 3, 9–12, 23–25, 30 April; 3–5, 7, 17–22, 29–30 May; 1, 3–6, 9–14, 18–23, 28–30 June (18–23 sr); 1–5, 8, 15, 29, 31 July (1–5, 8 sr); 3–5, 11–12, 22–23 August; 2–5, 10–11, 15–21, 28–29 September (2–5, 15 sr); 1–4, 10–13, 22–23 October; 1–3, 11–12, 17–18 November (1–3 sr).

T. MARQUAND: Born 30 March 1998. To be particularly noted this season at the north's premier meetings. His favourable periods are: 24–29 March; 1–5, 13, 18–20, 28 April (18–20 sr); 3–6, 13, 17, 25–28, 30 May (30 sr); 2–3, 6, 10–16, 23–28 June (10–16 sr); 1–4, 8, 12, 20–25, 30 July (25, 30 sr); 10–15, 19, 23, 31 August; 2–3, 9, 11, 21–25, 30 September (11, 30 sr); 5, 7, 12–13, 29 October (12–13 sr); 3–7, 14–15 November.

FAVOURABLE PERIODS FOR NATIONAL HUNT JOCKEYS

H. COBDEN: Born 5 November 1998. Likely to do well on longer chases, especially at the larger meetings. His favourable periods are: 3–5, 10–11, 17–22 January; 1, 8, 10, 13–14, 26 February (13, 26 sr); 3–6, 14–16, 22, 26–29 March (3–6, 22 sr); 1, 4, 13–16, 20, 26 April (13–16, 20 sr); 1–6, 21, 26–28 May (21 sr); 1, 8–10, 20, 24 June; 2, 11, 27–31 July; 11–14, 20–26 August (20–26 sr); 10, 13–16, 28 September; 9–11, 15–20, 30–31 October (30–31 sr); 1–2, 10–14, 26 November; 9, 14–16, 21 December.

B. HUGHES: Born 27 June 1985. Should have best results riding three-year-olds, especially in the middle of the year. His favourable periods are: 16, 24–27 January (24 sr); 3–5, 13–17, 21–23 February; 7–9, 13–18, 20–22, 31 March (13–18 sr); 11, 18, 22, 24, 29–30 April (29–30 sr); 7–16, 27–31 May (27 sr); 10–18, 22–24 June; 14–16, 27–31 July; 6, 11–14, 21–23 August; 1–3, 15–18, 21–26 September (3 sr); 8–12, 17, 24–27, 31 October (17 sr); 1–3, 18, 21, 27–30 November (18 sr); 4–7, 10, 22 December.

S. TWISTON-DAVIES: Born 15 October 1992. Should be a force to be reckoned with at chases, as opposed to hurdles, in 2025. His favourable periods are: 2–4, 10–11, 17–25 January; 8–10, 12–14, 26 February; 1–6, 14–16, 26–28 March (6, 28 sr); 5–8, 16–18, 23 April (5–8 sr); 1–3, 19–22, 28–30 May; 12–15, 17–20, 28 June; 1–5, 19–22, 27–31 July (19–22 sr): 5, 8, 12, 23–26 August; 9, 16, 26–28 September; 6, 10, 14–18, 22–25, 28–31 October; 4–10, 18–22, 24 November (4, 24 sr); 5–6, 16–18, 22 December (16–18 sr).

Toby Jones

© ITV/Shutterstock

Acclaimed actor Toby Jones has recently found himself front page news due to his role as Alan Bates in ITV's topical drama *Mr Bates vs The Post Office*. Based upon the true-life story of the false prosecution of hundreds of British sub-postmasters, the role required more than just acting – it called for sensitivity and the skill to bring one quiet but tenacious man to the screen – and his plight to the attention of millions. In turn, Toby Jones himself is very 'normal'; quite unlike the stereotypical film and TV celebrity, and this difference has much to do with the planetary positions at his birth.

Born Toby Edward Heslewood Jones in Hammersmith on 7 September 1966, he's an analytical Sun Virgo with Moon in curious Gemini. In many ways he's a textbook Virgo: practical, self-deprecating and responsible, yet the Sun, quick-thinking Mercury, rebellious Uranus and power-driven Pluto are all conjunct in this sign, indicating an intensity and unusual depth that always wants to get to the bottom of an issue and be right.

With Moon in Gemini there's an active and agile mind, able to think creatively around everyday problems. This makes him as sharp as a razor, but unable to relax: 'My relaxation is my job, and when I'm *not* working, I'm working … I find I'm always observing'. As a text-book Virgo he has said that working is addictive, and it is that urge not so much to achieve ambitions but to do a job well done that gives him an almost forensic attention to detail when researching and preparing screen roles, making him well-suited to the role of Mr Bates which required such in-depth preparation. With Venus and Mars in Leo, there's a certain amount of pride in love, in finding an exclusive relationship with someone to feel proud of and with whom to enjoy the good life.

Again, like a true Virgoan, Toby strikes others as being very down-to-earth, and what has kept his feet on the ground all these years is the helpful Jupiter–Saturn link called a trine. He'll need to be grounded this year as February 2025 may bring massive (perhaps unexpected) change with two harsh Saturn contacts to unreliable Uranus and intense Pluto. Although his career is likely to remain successful, tense situations may involve him directly or indirectly and will centre on family relationships. There will be a need to simplify life, culminating with the second Saturn return in late April which indicates either the end of an era (an important personal one) or a final chance at big change as he moves into late middle age. There's likely to be a feeling of something in life that he simply *must* fulfil before it is too late – by September it will be time to address this issue.

Old Moore's tips are a racing certainty

Racing with the Trainers in 2025

ASTROLOGICAL POINTERS TO POSSIBLE WINNING PERIODS

The astrologically compiled dates below are presented to race-goers in the hope that they will point the way to some successful winning periods during the 2025 racing season. Specially recommended = sr

FAVOURABLE PERIODS FOR FLAT-RACE TRAINERS

A. M. BALDING: Born 29 December 1972. Shorter courses, particularly in the north, ought to bring best results. His favourable periods are: 21–22, 29 March; 1–4, 9–12, 19–20, 27–30 April; 1–5, 9, 16, 25–30 May (16 sr); 2–3, 11–12, 26–29 June (11–12 sr); 4, 12–15, 20, 31 July (20, 31 sr); 1, 10–11, 19, 24–26 August; 1–2, 14–18, 27–30 September (27–30 sr); 3, 11–15, 21–22, 29 October (15 sr); 2–3, 15–16, 21–25 November.

C. JOHNSTON: Born 4 October 1990. Ought to succeed with any older horses, especially early in the season. His favourable periods are: 19, 23–24 March (23 sr); 8, 11–12, 25, 28–30 April (8, 25 sr); 2–3, 15–17, 22–26, 30–31 May; 1, 3, 14–16, 23–28 June (23 sr); 5–7, 14–18, 21–22, 29 July; 3–7, 15, 17–22, 30–31 August; 1–2, 4–6, 12, 14, 25 September; 1, 10–11, 17–19, 22–23 October (22 sr); 3, 15–16, 22–26 November.

M. APPLEBY: Born 30 July 1970. Should do best fielding three- and four-year-olds at southern races this season. His favourable periods are: 19, 28–29 March; 5, 8, 13–17, 20, 24–26 April (17, 20 sr); 13–16, 21–23, 31 May (13–16 sr); 2–6, 8–13, 21, 23 June (21, 23 sr); 1, 3–5, 12, 15, 28 July (15 sr); 3–5, 18–22, 25–30 August (25, 30 sr); 8, 10–13, 16–18, 27 September (10 sr); 10–11, 15, 23, 31 October (10 sr); 14–17, 23–25, 30 November (30 sr).

FAVOURABLE PERIODS FOR NATIONAL HUNT TRAINERS

P. F. NICHOLLS: Born 17 April 1962. Could do especially well in the Midlands with longer courses, particularly in autumn. His favourable periods are: 18–22, 25–26 January (26 sr); 2, 12–15, 21–25, 27 February; 6–9, 16, 20–22, 27 March; 5, 13–18, 23–26 April (23–26 sr); 3–4, 16–17, 22–26 May (26 sr); 6–10, 13–14, 21, 28 June; 11, 18, 27–29 July; 1–8, 13, 23–26, 31 August; 2, 10, 13–19, 28 September; 4–11, 19–21, 30–31 October (30–31 sr); 3, 10, 16–17, 30 November; 1, 4–7, 21 December.

N. HENDERSON: Born 10 December 1950. Likely to succeed best in the longer chases with three- and four-year-olds. His favourable periods are: 3, 7–10, 31 January (31 sr); 12–13, 20, 25–26 February; 4, 13–19, 28 March; 11–12, 22, 30 April (11–12 sr); 5, 9, 13, 23–30 May (5, 9 sr); 12–13, 20, 30 June (30 sr); 3–7, 15, 26–31 July; 2–4, 18, 26, 30 August; 2–3, 13, 16, 20, 23 September (2–3 sr); 8–11, 16, 19–22, 30–31 October (30–31 sr); 1–3, 10–12, 23–26 November (23 sr); 3, 10, 16–18 December (16–18 sr).

D. SKELTON: Born 9 April 1985. May see best results fielding three-year-olds at northern venues – at any time of the year. His favourable periods are: 3, 8, 12, 31 January (31 sr); 1–2, 10, 14–18, 23 February (1–2 sr); 15–17, 22, 27–30 March; 8–11, 19–20, 30 April (30 sr); 5–6, 15–19, 22–27 May (22 sr); 8–9, 19, 20–22, 28–30 June; 1–3, 13, 25–26, 31 July (31 sr); 9, 21–25, 29–31 August; 6, 11–16, 23–28 September; 1–2, 16, 19–20, 24–27 October; 4, 7, 11, 24–25 November; 11, 16, 24 December (16, 24 sr).

60

Please name FOULSHAM'S ALMANACK when replying to advertisers

Greyhound Racing Numbers for 2025

TRAP-NUMBER FORECASTS FOR POTENTIAL SUCCESS

Each area of the UK has a ruling planetary number, and each month of 2025 has a prominent fortunate planetary number. This forecast is based on a combination of those numbers to provide a list of the most propitious dates for betting and the trap numbers most likely to be successful.

The table gives the main areas of the UK and under each monthly heading, the first column shows the best dates for betting, and the second, shaded column gives the trap numbers for the winner and the second dog.

Whilst making no claim to infallibility, this forecast should offer those who enjoy an occasional jaunt to greyhound race meetings a way of aligning their activities with the best planetary influences and potentially increasing their success rate.

MEETING	JAN	FEB	MAR	APRIL	MAY	JUNE	JULY	AUG	SEPT	OCT	NOV	DEC
London	2–8 (1 2) 24–27 (2 6)	2–12 (1 2) 24–28 (2 4)	2–7 (2 5) 20–24 (1 2)	5–9 (1 6) 17–25 (3 4)	6–12 (2 4) 20–24 (4 5)	5–10 (2 5) 22–29 (1 3)	8–12 (1 3) 20–26 (1 2)	1–9 (2 4) 25–31 (1 4)	7–11 (1 5) 20–27 (3 6)	1–6 (1 4) 16–21 (3 5)	4–10 (3 5) 21–25 (1 6)	3–4 (2 6) 23–29 (3 4)
Birmingham	3–7 (4 6) 15–21 (1 4)	3–13 (1 2) 22–26 (4 5)	10–15 (3 5) 24–27 (1 6)	3–9 (1 6) 23–29 (1 3)	3–10 (3 4) 25–31 (1 2)	13–14 (3 5) 20–27 (3 4)	3–11 (2 4) 27–31 (5 6)	3–8 (1 5) 22–27 (3 5)	1–4 (2 6) 18–26 (1 2)	8–14 (1 4) 26–31 (3 5)	2–6 (2 3) 17–23 (2 5)	7–14 (3 4) 19–24 (4 6)
Manchester	1–6 (1 3) 26–31 (2 3)	7–11 (2 6) 23–26 (3 6)	6–13 (1 4) 21–29 (1 5)	2–10 (4 6) 18–22 (2 6)	1–9 (3 6) 18–26 (1 4)	4–11 (4 5) 26–30 (5 6)	2–8 (2 3) 16–22 (1 3)	9–13 (1 4) 18–24 (1 2)	6–10 (4 6) 22–27 (3 4)	1–8 (3 5) 19–25 (2 6)	4–10 (2 3) 18–23 (4 5)	5–9 (5 6) 26–31 (2 5)
Newcastle	10–15 (1 4) 20–25 (2 4)	4–11 (2 6) 21–27 (3 4)	9–14 (3 5) 26–31 (1 6)	6–10 (1 2) 17–22 (4 5)	8–13 (2 4) 19–23 (1 5)	2–8 (2 3) 22–27 (2 6)	1–4 (1 3) 28–31 (2 4)	2–12 (3 4) 20–28 (2 4)	6–11 (1 2) 27–31 (4 6)	11–15 (2 4) 22–26 (1 4)	8–12 (2 3) 21–28 (1 6)	11–14 (3 5) 27–30 (2 5)
Sheffield	1–4 (2 5) 19–24 (4 5)	4–11 (2 6) 22–25 (2 3)	1–5 (2 5) 24–29 (1 6)	5–14 (1 3) 22–27 (3 6)	9–14 (4 6) 20–28 (1 5)	2–10 (3 4) 25–30 (1 2)	1–4 (1 3) 16–22 (4 6)	11–14 (1 2) 21–27 (2 5)	10–13 (4 5) 25–29 (1 3)	4–11 (1 5) 17–22 (1 3)	1–4 (1 6) 20–24 (2 4)	8–12 (3 4) 19–25 (5 6)
Wales	1–12 (1 2) 15–19 (1 2)	4–11 (1 3) 21–22 (1 5)	5–10 (2 5) 12–19 (1 2)	1–5 (1 2) 18–25 (1 6)	1–7 (1 5) 15–21 (1 2)	8–11 (2 5) 17–20 (5 6)	1–8 (1 6) 19–22 (1 2 3)	8–11 (3 4) 17–21 (1 3)	2–9 (1 2) 20–29 (2 4)	10–15 (1 2) 22–30 (1 6)	4–6 (1 3) 18–24 (5 6)	1–6 (1 3) 21–30 (1 2)
South of England	4–15 (3 6) 20–25 (5 6)	2–11 (4 5) 21–24 (1 3)	1–10 (1 5) 27–31 (3 4)	9–12 (2 3) 20–25 (1 2)	8–13 (3 4) 18–22 (2 4)	11–17 (2 4) 16–28 (2 6)	11–14 (2 3) 23–29 (1 6)	7–11 (4 5) 25–31 (2 4)	4–9 (3 6) 19–23 (4 5)	8–14 (2 4) 21–27 (3 6)	1–8 (3 5) 24–30 (1 2)	11–14 (5 6) 26–31 (2 3)

Psychic Readings

To get a general psychic reading.
Call 020 8748 2720
£40.00 to D.Stevens.

The Free Spirits Club

Friends, pen pals, romance.
UK-Wide. No Internet needed.
Call for details: **01633 526523**

Old Moore's Almanack

is published each year in June and is available from all good newsagents and booksellers.

You can also obtain a copy from Foulsham, *The Old Barrel Store, Drayman's Lane, Marlow, Bucks SL7 2FF* (01628 400600).
You can also buy online at
www.foulsham.com or phone 01256 302699.

The science behind the Moon's effect on your garden

An Introduction to Lunar Gardening

Nearly everyone is aware that the Moon affects the tides' rise and fall, caused by gravitational pull and a consequent swelling in the earth's seas and oceans. The cycles of the Moon also affect plant growth from one new Moon to the next (called a Lunation) via a process called *geotropism*. Plants germinate and thrive as they respond to gravity and its magnetic pull, either upwards (in the stems and leaves) or downwards (in the roots). The phases observed from one New Moon to the next help us plot the appropriate times to sow and plant, as the phases of increased or decreased gravitational pull vary with the New Moon, First Quarter, Full Moon and Last Quarter. Lunar gardening simply takes advantage of this process.

BIODYNAMIC AND LUNAR GARDENING

Biodynamic gardening has a spiritual, holistic philosophy behind it. This is essentially our link with Mother Nature and her lunar rhythms. The modern Biodynamic Movement began with the Austrian philosopher Rudolf Steiner in 1924 when a collection of farmers came to him for a solution to the decline in the quality of soil (and the food it produced). He had a holistic solution for them – treat the land used for farming as an ecosystem, as a living being. The soil must be properly nourished, and synthetic pesticides or fertilizers must be avoided.

The so-called biodynamic calendar makes use of the lunar phases, or the Moon's location in the zodiac at any one time, with importance placed on the waxing or waning periods. The general rule is that plants appearing *above the ground* (like lettuce) ought to be sown, planted or transplanted during the *waxing* of the Moon; root plants that grow *beneath the ground* (like potatoes) should be sown, planted or transplanted during the *waning* of the Moon. The Moon's magnetic effect isn't just on the sea tides either, but on the groundwater table.

In 1957, one of Steiner's followers – the researcher Maria Thun – developed the notion that the Moon's position in the zodiac might be a reliable basis to work from. She was soon looking to the qualities of the Four Elements of Greek Philosophy: Fire, Earth, Air and Water. She then correlated them with various types of plant, namely a Fruit or Seed type (Fire), a Root type (Earth), a Flower type (Air) and a Leaf type (Water). These, respectively, correspond to Aries, Leo, Sagittarius (Fire); Taurus, Virgo, Capricorn (Earth); Gemini, Libra, Aquarius (Air) and Cancer, Scorpio, Pisces (Water). By 1963, she had published a report of her findings.

Today, biodynamic farms use the rather eyebrow-raising homeopathic compound known as 'Preparation 500'. This is created by stuffing a cow horn with manure and then burying it under the soil in autumn, to be retrieved the next spring. The result is a robust compost, rich in calcium compounds which greatly enhances the structure of the soil, and curbs levels of acidity. We've come a long way since those lectures by Steiner and now Biodynamic agriculture is used by professional farmers across the world. Whether you've a window box, a few square feet of garden or an allotment, give lunar gardening a try. It has proven results.

James Lynn Page (www.astro.nu)

Harness the power of the Moon in your garden

Best Sowing And Planting Times for the Garden in 2025

WHEN TO PLANT OR SOW BY THE MOON TO GET THE BEST RESULTS

Peas, beans, flowering vegetables and plants which produce fruit above the ground should always be sown under a waxing Moon (the period from New Moon to Full). Potatoes and root crops should always be sown when the Moon is low and below the Earth. If you sow, plant or re-pot at the times set out below, it is reasonably certain you will have really fine results. The times are Greenwich Mean Time. Allowances must be made for British Summer Time.

Month	Day	Planting Times			
JANUARY	12, 13, 14 28, 29, 30	8.45 to 11.10 am 8.10 to 11.55 am	1.55 to 2.45 pm 1.05 to 2.50 pm		
FEBRUARY	11, 12, 13 26, 27, 28	8.40 to 10.55 am 8.15 to 10.15 am	12.25 to 2.40 pm 1.10 to 3.50 pm		
		Begin sowing legumes, leaf vegetables and root vegetables. Delay beetroot until the weather is mild. Cut early kidney potatoes for seed and use a heater or heat mats to get them started.			
MARCH	13, 14, 15 28, 29, 30	8.00 to 11.50 am 8.10 am to 1.00 pm	1.00 to 2.10 pm 1.15 to 2.30 pm	2.55 to 4.10 pm 3.00 to 4.10 pm	
		Planting and sowing into the ground can begin this month. Sow asparagus, celery, brassicas, and continue with root vegetables and legumes. Cabbages, onion sets and sea-kale may be planted out.			
APRIL	12, 13, 14 25, 27, 28	7.00 to 11.25 am 7.20 to 11.10 am	1.00 to 2.25 pm 12.45 to 3.00 pm	4.00 to 5.05 pm 4.05 to 5.40 pm	
		Sowing of tomatoes and peppers can begin indoors. Continue sowing legumes, brassicas and leaf vegetables for the main summer crop. Plant out rhubarb, artichokes, asparagus and small salad vegetables. Tie up lettuce and in dry weather water seed in beds.			
MAY	11, 12, 13 26, 27, 28	7.10 to 11.45 am 7.40 to 11.20 am	1.10 pm to 2.25 pm 12.05 to 2.30 pm	4.15 to 5.55 pm 4.00 to 5.35 pm	
		Sow cucumber, dwarf bean, runner beans and courgettes and a full crop of kidney beans. Transplant cabbage, winter greens, cauliflower and celery seedlings. Hoe and stake peas, water newly planted crops.			
JUNE	10, 11, 12 24, 25, 26	7.10 to 11.00 am 7.40 to 10.50 am	12.40 to 3.00 pm 12.40 to 2.25 pm	4.15 to 5.50 pm 4.15 to 5.55 pm	
		Top beans and peas to assist the filling of the pods. Set kidney beans. Thin out onions, leeks, parsnips and early turnips. Plant tomatoes and peppers outdoors. Water all crops well during dry spells.			
JULY	9, 10, 11 23, 24, 25	7.15 to 11.20 am 7.20 to 11.05 am	12.35 to 3.35 pm 12.50 to 3.15 pm	4.25 to 6.25 pm 4.50 to 7.25 pm	
		Plant out the last of the brassicas and cabbages and earth up celery. Lift full-grown winter onions and new potatoes. Pick vine crops as they ripen to encourage new fruit.			
AUGUST	8, 9, 10 22, 23, 24	7.05 to 11.10 am 7.15 to 11.20 am	12.30 to 3.15 pm 12.45 to 3.05 pm	6.00 to 8.20 pm 6.15 to 8.25 pm	
		Sow early cabbages and parsley for the succeeding year, also spinach, broccoli and cauliflower to stand the winter and transplant seedlings. Continue to pick legumes and vine crops as they ripen.			
SEPTEMBER	6, 7, 8 20, 21, 22	6.55 to 11.25 am 7.25 to 11.35 am	1.10 to 4.25 pm 12.50 to 3.55 pm	6.00 to 8.00 pm 5.45 to 7.10 pm	
		Plant some radishes, early cabbages, cauliflower, and some herbs like mint, thyme and tarragon in frames for winter use. Sow the last winter lettuce. Harvest crops before any risk of frost.			
OCTOBER	6, 7, 8 20, 21, 22	8.00 to 11.55 am 8.10 to 11.15 am	1.10 to 3.25 pm 1.05 to 3.55 pm	4.50 to 6.40 pm 4.15 to 5.55 pm	
		Plant some radishes, early cabbages, cauliflower, and some herbs like mint, thyme and tarragon in frames for winter use. Sow the last winter lettuce. Harvest crops before any risk of frost.			
NOVEMBER	4, 5, 6 19, 20, 21	8.10 am to 12.10 pm 8.50 am to 12.05 pm	1.55 to 4.30 pm 2.20 to 4.00 pm		
		Dig ground once crops are carried off and there is no intention to plant again until spring. Shallots are readily propagated by offcuts. Clear fallen leaves quickly and dispose of diseased plants.			
DECEMBER	3, 4, 5 19, 20, 21	9.10 am to 1.20 pm 9.00 am to 12.40 pm	2.30 to 3.05 pm 2.00 to 3.15 pm		
		Earth up celery. Sow small salad vegetables in warm borders covered with mats.			

Old Moore selects the teams

Football Pools Forecast for 2025

This forecast, based on a combination of planetary indications and team colours, lists the teams likely to draw on the dates given, or within two days either side. No claims to infallibility are made and readers should use their own judgement, but forecasts may help them in the final selection.

4 January
Lincoln City, Norwich, Preston, Manchester Utd, Bristol City

11 January
Wigan, Liverpool, Manchester City, Kilmarnock, Brentford

18 January
Brighton, Chelsea, Aberdeen, Burnley, Reading, Spurs

25 January
Everton, Blackburn Rovers, Stoke City, Preston, West Bromwich Albion

1 February
Swansea, Kilmarnock, Sheffield Wednesday, Liverpool, Birmingham

8 February
Newcastle Utd, Chelsea, West Ham, Stockport, Shrewsbury Town

15 February
Stockport County, Wigan, Celtic, Stoke City, Leicester

22 February
Derby County, Motherwell, Oxford Utd, Manchester Utd, Bristol City

1 March
Southampton, Wrexham, Burnley, Spurs, Bournemouth

8 March
Manchester City, Cardiff City, Coventry City, Swansea City, Peterborough

15 March
Celtic, Spurs, Aberdeen, Brentford, West Bromwich Albion, Swindon

22 March
Wolves, Coventry City, Reading, Liverpool, Wigan

29 March
Leicester, Rangers, Hull, Bolton, Southampton, West Ham

5 April
West Ham, Cardiff City, Wolves, Cambridge Utd, Swansea City

12 April
Manchester Utd, Derby County, Celtic, Bournemouth, Newcastle Utd

19 April
Portsmouth, Manchester City, Manchester Utd, Aston Villa, Bolton

26 April
Blackburn Rovers, Cardiff City, Preston, West Bromwich Albion, Portsmouth

3 May
QPR, Sunderland, Middlesbrough, Millwall, Wrexham, Leeds

10 May
Port Vale, Preston, Swindon, Blackpool, Barnsley, Stevenage

17 May
Dundee Utd, Leeds, Wolves, Port Vale, Arsenal

24 May
Blackpool, Liverpool, Hibernian, Peterborough, Burnley

16 August
Aberdeen, Everton, Spurs, Manchester Utd, Cardiff City

23 August
Brighton, Crystal Palace, Fulham, Notts County, Bolton

30 August
Manchester City, Ipswich Town, Celtic, Hearts, MK Dons, Huddersfield

6 September
Blackpool, Chelsea, Leicester, Motherwell, Crystal Palace

13 September
Blackburn Rovers, Stoke City, Charlton Athletic, Birmingham

20 September
Bristol City, Ross County, Middlesbrough, Preston, Aston Villa

27 September
Crystal Palace, Arsenal, Bournemouth, Fulham, West Ham

4 October
Norwich, Everton, Bristol Rovers, Bolton, West Ham

11 October
Southampton, Leeds Utd, Northampton, Newcastle Utd, Bolton

18 October
West Bromwich Albion, Stevenage, Rangers, Newcastle Utd, Oxford Utd

25 October
Arsenal, Bristol Rovers, Lincoln City, West Bromwich Albion

1 November
Manchester City, Everton, Spurs, Coventry City, Sheffield Utd

8 November
Everton, Blackburn Rovers, Spurs, Stoke City, Chelsea

15 November
Fulham, Huddersfield, Leicester, Rotherham Utd, Sheffield Utd

22 November
Stevenage, Shrewsbury Town, Lincoln City, West Ham, Aberdeen

29 November
Southampton, Crystal Palace, Coventry City, Bolton, Reading

6 December
Stockport, QPR, Watford, Sunderland, Crystal Palace

13 December
Liverpool, Bristol Rovers, Manchester Utd, Peterborough, Wolves

20 December
Leyton Orient, Charlton Athletic, Burnley, Brighton, Derby County

27 December Stevenage, Leicester, Wigan, Norwich, Everton

 # Angler's Guide for 2025
THE BEST DATES AND TECHNIQUES FOR SUCCESSFUL FISHING

JANUARY: Sport can be hard due to low temperatures, so stick to deeper water on rivers and lakes. Backwaters are a good bet when main rivers are flooded: try float or leger tactics in slack water swims. Shoaling cod may be caught from the beaches, especially in Scotland, on casting gear but they will soon thin out as temperatures rise. **Best days:** 6, 8 (am), 9 (pm), 13, 16 (pm), 25, 26, 28 (am), 30, 31 (pm).

FEBRUARY: Predator fishing offers the best action with pike, perch and zander all possible on fish baits, but scale down your tackle if the temperature plummets. Big chub can also be had on leger tactics. Spring salmon on the cards for some anglers, but beach rods will have to work harder for their catches. Flatties will still feature, although bigger fish can be had when afloat. **Best days:** 2, 5 (pm), 7, 9 (am), 13, 17 (am), 22, 26, 25, 26 (pm).

MARCH: The freshwater river season closes this month, but almost all commercial still waters will stay open. If mild weather comes early, head for sheltered lakes which can produce superb mixed catches of roach, bream, carp and even tench. Trout anglers head for deep, still waters from the 15th. **Best days:** 1, 2, 3, 7 (am), 14, 15, 16 (pm), 21, 22 (am), 26, 27, 31 (pm).

APRIL: Beach anglers can enjoy the spring run of codling, while those fishing wrecks can expect bumper hauls of pollack, ling and occasional big cod on artificial baits. Ray fishing good, especially in the Solent. Most flies will take trout on still waters but a more careful approach is needed in rivers. **Best days:** 4, 5 (pm), 9, 10, 11 (am), 15, 18, 20 (pm), 27, 29, 30 (am).

MAY: Crab baits worthy for early school bass, flounder and eel, while ragworm and lugworm will take their fair share of plaice in harbours and estuaries. Still-water trout should respond to warmer weather and can be taken on floating lines. Carp will be the bulk of catches for commercial still-water anglers. **Best days:** 1, 2, 9, 11 (am), 13, 16 (pm), 21, 23 (pm), 28, 29, 30 (am).

JUNE: The Glorious 16th will enable specimen tench, carp and bream to be targeted with big baits on both float and leger tackle. Rivers with more pace should provide excellent catches of roach and chub. Beach anglers will find bass more widespread, while their boat counterparts can expect mackerel – the perfect bait for shark and tope – which will start to show off many southern and Welsh ports. **Best days:** 2, 6, 9 (pm), 16, 17, 18 (am), 20, 24 (am), 27, 28 (pm).

JULY: Top sport on rivers and lakes with virtually all species responsive, mostly to particle baits such as corn, hemp and tares. Try swims with plenty of flow as fish, particularly barbel and bream, will be hungry for oxygen-rich water during hot weather. Evening sessions ideal for fly anglers pursuing trout. Shy mullet may be tempted during quiet days around harbours, and bass will be bigger. **Best days:** 1, 3, 6 (am), 9, 11 (am), 12, 14, 15 (pm), 19, 21, 26, 31 (pm).

AUGUST: Low oxygen levels suggest fishing either very early morning or evening periods. Sea anglers afloat can look forward to a multitude of species including bream, bass, pollack, conger and gurnard. Fresh fish baits and crab will outscore all others. **Best days:** 2, 3, 6, 7 (pm), 11, 14, 16 (pm), 22, 24 (am), 28, 30, 31 (pm).

SEPTEMBER: Fish will have had time to feed well and big specimens can be expected. Barbel, roach, bream, tench and chub will all be at their optimum weight. Trout anglers may struggle to locate decent fish, although beach and boat rods will be hunting big bass with sand eel baits, crab or lures. **Best days:** 3, 4, 9, 11 (am), 14, 18 (pm), 22, 23 (am), 27, 28, 30 (pm).

OCTOBER: Cooler temperatures may mean slow sport on lakes, but rivers will be at their peak for roach, chub and dace on caster or maggot. Float tactics are good but don't discount leger or feeder gear. Beach anglers expect the first of the winter codling, where lugworm and squid will be top baits. Extra water may prompt decent catches of salmon for game anglers. **Best days:** 2, 3, 4 (am), 10, 12 (pm), 18, 19 (pm), 22, 24, 25, 30, 31 (pm).

NOVEMBER: With shorter days, codling will come closer inshore, especially at deeper venues such as steep beaches, harbour walls and piers. Bad weather may mean slower sport for coarse anglers, who need to scale down hooks and baits. Predator hunters can expect big pike on baits rather than lures. **Best days:** 3, 5, 9, 10 (pm), 14, 15 (pm), 20, 21 (am), 26, 27, 28 (am).

DECEMBER: A roving approach is best during colder weather. Try different swims on backwaters, where roach will take bread flake, and chub can be had on cheese paste, bread, worms and cockles. Pin baits hard to the bottom or let them roll in the flow. After a storm is ideal for targeting codling on beaches, when they attack food stirred up by rough weather. Try night sessions for greater success. **Best days:** 1, 2, 10, 11 (am), 14, 15 (am), 19, 20 (pm), 26, 27 (am), 30, 31 (pm).

Lucky Dates to Play Bingo in 2025
CHECK YOUR ZODIAC SIGN FOR YOUR GOOD-LUCK TIMES

Aries (Birthdays 21 March to 20 April)
24 January to 22 March, 22 July to 27 August, 30 September to 1 December

❋

Taurus (Birthdays 21 April to 21 May)
27 February to 2 April, 27 June to 14 September, 4 November to 22 December

❋

Gemini (Birthdays 22 May to 21 June)
5 January to 22 March, 22 May to 27 July, 2 October to 25 November

❋

Cancer (Birthdays 22 June to 22 July)
10 February to 24 April, 21 July to 21 September, 4 November to 15 December

❋

Leo (Birthdays 23 July to 23 August)
4 March to 22 May, 7 July to 24 September, 24 November to 28 December

❋

Virgo (Birthdays 24 August to 23 September)
17 February to 12 April, 12 July to 1 September, 2 November to 29 December

❋

Libra (Birthdays 24 September to 23 October)
2 January to 7 February, 23 April to 21 June, 4 September to 30 November

❋

Scorpio (Birthdays 24 October to 22 November)
25 February to 2 April, 29 June to 2 September, 24 November to 22 December

❋

Sagittarius (Birthdays 23 November to 21 December)
13 February to 17 April, 14 June to 19 August, 27 October to 4 December

❋

Capricorn (Birthdays 22 December to 20 January)
14 January to 22 March, 31 May to 4 July, 23 October to 29 November

❋

Aquarius (Birthdays 21 January to 19 February)
2 January to 1 March, 2 May to 24 July, 12 October to 28 November

❋

Pisces (Birthdays 20 February to 20 March)
27 February to 29 April, 5 July to 2 September, 17 November to 21 December

Please name FOULSHAM'S ALMANACK when replying to advertisers

Thunderball Astro-Guide for 2025

Thunderball forecasts are based on the power of the Sun and Jupiter in each zodiacal period. In a random draw there can be no guarantee, but these numbers may help to improve your chances. First, find your Sun sign in the left-hand column. Then read across the first panel to select five numbers 1–39 for the main part of your entry. Then select one number from the second panel for the Thunderball.

ARIES 21 MARCH TO 20 APRIL	5	6	10	23	31	34	4	7	8	13
TAURUS 21 APRIL TO 21 MAY	7	18	19	22	27	39	2	5	12	14
GEMINI 22 MAY TO 21 JUNE	2	4	11	20	32	38	6	7	8	13
CANCER 22 JUNE TO 22 JULY	1	8	13	24	31	36	2	4	10	12
LEO 23 JULY TO 23 AUGUST	5	9	16	20	29	32	1	6	8	11
VIRGO 24 AUGUST TO 23 SEPTEMBER	2	4	10	23	30	33	3	5	9	13
LIBRA 24 SEPTEMBER TO 23 OCTOBER	4	5	18	22	23	29	2	6	8	12
SCORPIO 24 OCTOBER TO 22 NOVEMBER	7	12	21	23	34	35	4	7	10	11
SAGITTARIUS 23 NOVEMBER TO 21 DECEMBER	4	7	14	26	30	33	1	3	7	12
CAPRICORN 22 DECEMBER TO 20 JANUARY	5	8	9	11	26	29	3	6	7	11
AQUARIUS 21 JANUARY TO 19 FEBRUARY	6	11	12	24	27	31	2	8	9	10
PISCES 20 FEBRUARY TO 20 MARCH	2	6	9	17	24	39	2	4	11	13

THE SPELL LADY
35 years' experience

I can provide advice for white magik spells and rituals for romance, love, find a soul-mate, good luck, hex/curse removals, remote healing, and many more. Most things can be solved with a white magik spell.

Please contact me on: **01303 890542** or **07933 962544**
alstroud@btinternet.com

Who wants to be a millionaire…?

Your Lucky Lotto

The prevailing planetary influences are the basis for this astro-guide to lucky Lotto numbers in 2025. Any Lotto forecast must be fallible, but to give yourself the best chance of winning, refer to the section on your birth sign.

 ## ARIES
BORN 21 MARCH TO 20 APRIL

Neptune, the planet of dreams and mysticism, visits Aries this year – in fact, for a lengthy stay. Don't underestimate the strength of personal intuition when playing the lottery; listen to your inner ear if you have a strange feeling that certain numbers are calling you. You may also consider choosing numbers connected with means of communication, such as telephone numbers or those related to transport, perhaps your car, local bus or train.

2	8	17	18	28	30	41	42	48	52
9	11	20	26	33	38	44	45	53	57

 ## TAURUS
BORN 21 APRIL TO 21 MAY

Usually conservative in behaviour, and one who can be relied upon to be predictable, this year turn all that on its head when it comes to playing the lottery and do things differently. Change is the key over the coming twelve months as eccentric Uranus passes through your sign so just go with whatever you feel like. For an additional indicator to potential lottery wealth, try numbers linked to your personal possessions or bank account.

3	7	17	27	36	38	44	45	49	51
9	13	29	30	32	43	46	47	58	59

 ## LEO
BORN 23 JULY TO 23 AUGUST

Pluto occupies your 'marriage house' this year, and since Pluto is traditionally associated with wealth and big business, any close partnerships might be of significant benefit to you in your approach to the lottery. In short, let *them* choose the numbers! If you're not currently in a relationship or any kind of partnership, you could also choose numbers connected with an old friendship or a regular social group.

2	5	9	10	20	22	29	31	43	48
6	8	15	16	23	26	37	42	55	56

 ## VIRGO
BORN 24 AUGUST TO 23 SEPTEMBER

Virgo is the ultimate realist of the zodiac, and therefore you should be happy to use all the rational logic at your disposal in your approach to the lottery this year. Your chart suggests that playing with a partner or friend or varying the numbers each week could be successful. Be creative! Alternatively, you could try selecting numbers connected with your chosen career – especially your current employer, or also those connected with your mother.

4	6	16	21	33	38	44	47	53	56
7	9	22	27	39	41	48	50	57	59

 ## SAGITTARIUS
BORN 23 NOVEMBER TO 21 DECEMBER

Astrologers know that Sagittarius is the luckiest sign in the zodiac, although this is really about intuition and faith in tomorrow. Certainly, you've an uncanny feel for the right moment when it comes to taking chances so maybe this year this will mean an instinct for lottery numbers. In 2025 your chart indicates that you should play the lottery with a partner, or otherwise choose numbers connected to them or a close friend, or perhaps even a rival!

3	9	14	15	24	28	32	37	45	52
10	12	17	22	29	30	38	43	55	56

 ## CAPRICORN
BORN 22 DECEMBER to 20 JANUARY

There are multiple astrological reasons in your chart for you to retain your usual virtues of caution and consistency this year. If you have a favoured set of numbers, retain them. You could also draw up a fresh set of numbers and then keep to *them*. For an astrological pointer to those numbers Capricorn, you could consider numbers linked to your job, your doctor, or a place of work. Who knows, it might be your turn!

1	2	13	15	21	30	42	48	55	56
6	8	16	20	36	37	49	50	58	59

...You do! Let Old Moore guide your choice

Astro-guide for 2025

Choose two numbers from the first square, then one number from each of the following squares. Either keep to the same numbers each week or vary the astrological indicators according to your personal vibrations.

USING THIS SYSTEM READER WINS **£40,000** MRS THERESE SINGER OF GLASGOW

GEMINI
BORN 22 MAY TO 21 JUNE

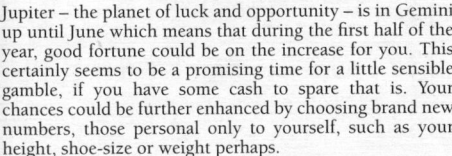

Jupiter – the planet of luck and opportunity – is in Gemini up until June which means that during the first half of the year, good fortune could be on the increase for you. This certainly seems to be a promising time for a little sensible gamble, if you have some cash to spare that is. Your chances could be further enhanced by choosing brand new numbers, those personal only to yourself, such as your height, shoe-size or weight perhaps.

3	9	22	24	36	39	47	48	55	57
11	17	28	30	40	41	50	54	58	59

CANCER
BORN 22 JUNE TO 22 JULY

Jupiter (the planet of good fortune) occupies Cancer from July through until the end of the year. This could well turn into a phase when the odds at gambling or taking chances, including playing the lottery, are significantly improved. And that's an understatement! For the numbers themselves, try some that are especially connected to your recent past, or alternatively to a hospital familiar to you.

10	12	25	26	30	31	42	45	50	51
17	18	28	29	33	39	47	49	56	59

LIBRA
BORN 24 SEPTEMBER TO 23 OCTOBER

This year, unstable, unreliable Neptune will be in your solar seventh house of partnerships so, although you're always focused on relationships generally, the broad advice this year is to avoid playing the lottery with partners or in syndicates. Get ready to be more selfish! Alternatively, any numbers linked to places of learning, now or in the past, religious worship, or also a foreign holiday are meaningful for you in 2025.

1	6	15	16	26	27	32	35	52	53
7	11	22	23	29	30	41	44	57	58

SCORPIO
24 OCTOBER TO 22 NOVEMBER

As a Water sign you are naturally intuitive and this year you should watch for the uncanny and allow the Universe to leave its 'messages' for you. Be open-minded to allow the planets to guide you in your daily life – some numbers might pop up at unexpected moments. Alternatively, choose numbers connected with business or finance, such as bank details, NI or tax numbers, and in particular any *joint* bank accounts you have.

3	7	11	17	32	33	41	43	53	54
8	10	22	29	36	38	45	50	56	57

AQUARIUS
BORN 21 JANUARY TO 19 FEBRUARY

Pluto, traditionally associated with wealth, continues through your sign in 2025 and, since this planet often indicates financial advantage, perhaps this means life changing money is on its way? Old Moore would suggest that changing your numbers each week, rather than keeping favourite ones, is advised. Your astrologically favoured numbers this year are those connected to a romantic partner, your children, pets or a creative project.

1	6	17	19	34	38	43	48	52	56
13	14	22	27	39	40	49	50	57	58

PISCES
BORN 20 FEBRUARY TO 20 MARCH

Saturn, the great taskmaster of the zodiac, is presently travelling through Pisces, which suggests you should try keeping to numbers you normally use when playing the lottery. It's consistency that he's after, and if you've ever had a win in the past, do use those same numbers again. As an additional pointer for the next twelve months, select numbers linked to your home, family background or your father.

12	14	25	26	35	39	44	46	49	50
20	21	31	34	40	42	47	48	52	56

Hit the Jackpot with Old Moore!

Euro Millions Astro-indicator for 2025

Twelve has always been the perfect 'cyclical' number and is the 'pool' from which you can select from numbers below – they may help to improve your chances. Find your Sun sign in the left-hand column, then read across the first panel and choose five numbers (1–50) for the main board. Then, two for the Lucky Star section on the right. Some will overlap.

ARIES 21 March to 20 April	14	24	26	31	35	39	43	44	7	8	10	11
TAURUS 21 April to 21 May	1	10	14	22	33	36	37	48	4	6	10	12
GEMINI 22 May to 21 June	9	15	27	30	37	40	42	43	1	4	8	9
CANCER 22 June to 22 July	7	16	26	28	31	39	42	49	2	5	6	7
LEO 23 July to 23 August	2	12	15	28	32	33	43	48	1	5	9	10
VIRGO 24 August to 23 September	8	14	27	29	32	40	41	50	3	6	12	13
LIBRA 24 September to 23 October	16	19	26	33	38	42	44	45	5	6	11	12
SCORPIO 24 October to 22 November	1	3	7	12	30	31	40	49	2	3	7	11
SAGITTARIUS 23 November to 21 December	6	8	15	18	20	25	42	47	1	2	8	13
CAPRICORN 22 December to 20 January	8	9	30	32	38	40	42	46	1	4	10	12
AQUARIUS 21 January to 19 February	2	6	13	19	27	28	38	50	2	5	8	9
PISCES 20 February to 20 March	4	10	18	27	30	34	45	49	1	4	9	10

Back by popular demand, Foulsham Publishing are proud to present this complete guide to gardening in harmony with the rhythm of the moon. Gardeners at RHS Wisley have proved the benefits of the lunar effect, which produces higher yields and better flavour in vegetables, and stronger, more colourful flower beds. Everything you need to know about the position of the moon and the planets through the year is here, plus a 15-month calendar and timetable.

£9.99

Published August 2024

978-0-572-04850-1   30% discount on-line at www.foulsham.com or by calling 01256 302699 with code OM4.

Health Lottery Astro-guide for 2025

Health Lottery forecasts are based on the strength of Jupiter and planetary associations with the solar sixth house. These aspects are traditionally connected to health matters, whilst Jupiter signifies good luck generally. The numbers below may help to improve your chances at winning: just find your Sun sign, then select three numbers 1–50 from the first panel. Then choose two from the second 1–30.

Sign	Dates	First panel (1–50)	Second panel (1–30)
ARIES	21 March to 20 April	8 9 30 37 43 49	7 8 16 24
TAURUS	21 April to 21 May	2 3 15 32 40 46	6 18 24 28
GEMINI	22 May to 21 June	11 21 24 33 39 43	5 10 14 25
CANCER	22 June to 22 July	14 20 29 32 38 45	8 11 22 30
LEO	23 July to 23 August	9 13 14 23 41 48	6 12 13 25
VIRGO	24 August to 23 September	10 17 25 28 39 50	7 15 20 29
LIBRA	24 September to 23 October	12 13 20 33 34 40	3 5 9 24
SCORPIO	24 October to 22 November	2 6 11 31 42 47	4 17 26 30
SAGITTARIUS	23 November to 21 December	11 15 18 27 40 41	7 16 23 25
CAPRICORN	22 December to 20 January	16 22 30 32 37 49	14 20 28 29
AQUARIUS	21 January to 19 February	1 12 19 26 35 37	4 15 22 24
PISCES	20 February to 20 March	4 10 25 41 44 45	2 11 21 30

THE BEST WINES IN THE SUPERMARKETS

Select the wine that suits your mood.

The top wine buyers are now in the supermarkets so that's where the most characterful wines are on offer. These tasting teams buy the pick of the world's vintages and offer a broad range of superb wines. This guide helps to direct your choice.

£9.99

Published August 2024

30% discount on-line at www.foulsham.com or by calling 01256 302699 with code OM2. Also available from good bookshops.

978-0-572-04849-5

The Oldest Annual Publication...

UK Fairs and Events 2025

Dates are based on traditional fixtures and both dates and venues are subject to change. Always check local press, online or with the organisers well in advance.

AGRICULTURAL AND COUNTRYSIDE

Anglesey County Show: Gwalchmai 12–13 August
Appleby Horse Fair: Appleby-in-Westmorland, Cumbria 5–11 June
Bakewell Show: 6–7 August
Bingley Show: Myrtle Park, Bingley 19 July
Black Isle Show: Mansfield Showground, Muir of Ord 7 August
Border Union Show: Springwood Park, Kelso 25–26 July
Cheshire County Show: Tabley, Nr Knutsford 17–18 June
Country Fest: Westmorland County Showground, Lane Farm, Crooklands, Milnthorpe 31 May–1 June
Countryside Live: Great Yorkshire Showground, Harrogate 18–19 October
Cumberland County Show: Rickerby Park, Carlisle 14 June
Denbigh and Flint Show: The Green, Denbigh 21 August
Derbyshire County Show: Elvaston, Nr Derby 22 June
Devon County Show: Westpoint, Clyst St Mary, Exeter 15–17 May
Dorset County Show: Dorchester Showground 6–7 September
Dumfries and Lockerbie Agricultural Show: Park Farm, Dumfries 2 August
East of England Autumn Show: Showground, Peterborough 12 October
East of England Show and Just Dogs Live: Showground, Peterborough 4–6 July
Edenbridge and Oxted Agricultural Show: Ardenrun Showground, Lingfield 25 August
Eye Show: Goodrich Park, Palgrave 24–25 August
Great Yorkshire Show: Great Yorkshire Showground, Harrogate 8–11 July
Hertfordshire County Show: The Showground, Redbourn 24–25 May
Kelso Ram Sales: Springwood Park 12 September
Kent County Show: Detling, Maidstone 4–6 July (provisional)
Lincolnshire Show: Grange-de-Lings, Lincoln 18–19 June
Monmouthshire Show: Vauxhall Fields, Monmouth 28 August

Nantwich Show and International Cheese Awards: Dorfold Hall Park, Nantwich 30 July
New Forest and Hampshire County Show: New Park, Brockenhurst 29–31 July
Newark and Nottinghamshire County Show: Newark Showground, Newark-on-Trent 10–11 May
Newark Vintage Tractor and Heritage Show: Showground, Newark-on-Trent 8–9 November
North Somerset Show: Bathing Pond Fields, Wraxall, Nr Bristol 5 May
Northumberland County Show: Bywell, Nr Stocksfield 26 May
Oxfordshire County and Thame Show: Thame Showground 26 July
Pembrokeshire County Show: Withybush, Haverfordwest 19–21 August
Romsey Show: Broadlands, Romsey 13 September
Royal Bath & West AMES: Showground, Shepton Mallet 5 February
Royal Bath & West Dairy Show: Showground, Shepton Mallet 1 October
Royal Bath & West Show: Showground, Shepton Mallet 28–31 May (provisional)
Royal Cornwall Show: Wadebridge 5–7 June
Royal County of Berkshire Show: Newbury Showground 20–21 September
Royal Highland Show: Ingliston, Edinburgh 19–22 June (provisional)
Royal Norfolk Show: Norfolk Showground, Norwich 25–26 June
Royal Welsh Show: Llanelwedd, Builth Wells 21–24 July
Royal Welsh Winter Fair: Llanelwedd, Builth Wells 24–25 November
Shire Horse Society Spring Show: Arena UK Showground, Allington 21–23 March
Shropshire County Show: West Midlands Agricultural Showground, Shrewsbury 31 May
South of England Autumn Show and Horse Trials: SoE Centre, Haywards Heath 20–21 September
South of England Show: South of England Centre, Ardingly, Haywards Heath 6–8 June (provisional)
Staffordshire County Show: Stafford Showground 28–29 May
Suffolk Show: Trinity Park, Ipswich 28–29 May

Surrey County Show: Stoke Park, Guildford 26 May
Tendring Hundred Show: Lawford House Park, Nr Manningtree 12 July
Turriff Show: The Showground, Turriff, Aberdeenshire 3–4 August
Westmorland County Show: Lane Farm, Crooklands 11 September

OTHER EVENTS

Badminton Horse Trials: 7–11 May
BBC Gardeners' World Live: NEC Birmingham 12–15 June (provisional)
Blackpool Illuminations: End Aug 2025–early January 2026 (check local press for dates)
Border Union Championship Dog Show: Springwood Park, Kelso 21–22 June
Braemar Gathering: 6 September
Burghley Horse Trials: Burghley Park, 4–7 September (provisional)
Chester Folk Festival: Kelsall 25–26 May
Cowes Week: 2–8 August
Crufts Dog Show: NEC Birmingham 6–9 March
Edinburgh International Festival: 1–25 August
Edinburgh Military Tattoo: Edinburgh Castle Esplanade 1–23 August
Glastonbury Festival: 25–29 June (provisional)
Golf. British Open Championship: Royal Portrush 13–20 July. **Women's British Open**: Royal Porthcawl August, date unconfirmed. **Senior Open**: Royal Portrush 13–20 July. For Amateurs, Boys and Girls Championships check www.randa.org
Hay Festival: Hay-on-Wye 22 May–1 June
Helston Furry Dance: 8 May
Henley Regatta: 1–6 July (provisional)
The Hoppings (funfair): Town Moor, Newcastle 20–28 June
Horse Racing. Cheltenham Gold Cup: 14 March. **Grand National**: Aintree 5 April. **Scottish Grand National**: Ayr 19 April. **2000 Guineas**: Newmarket 3 May. **Epsom Derby**: 7 June. **Royal Ascot**: 17–21 June. **Glorious Goodwood**: 22–26 July. **St Leger**: Doncaster 13 September. **King George VI Chase**: Kempton 26 December.
Hull Fair: 10–18 October
Isle of Man TT Races: Douglas, IoM 26 May–8 June
Isle of Wight Festival: Seaclose Park, Newport, Isle of Wight 19–22 June
Jersey Battle of Flowers: 8–10 August
Leeds Festival: Bramham Park 22–24 August
Llangollen International Musical Eisteddfod: 17 June–12 July (provisional)
London to Brighton Veteran Car Run: Hyde Park, London–Madeira Drive, Brighton 2 November
London Harness Horse Parade: South of England Showground, Ardingly, Haywards Heath 21 April
London Marathon: Greenwich Park–The Mall, London 27 April
Lord Mayor's Show: City of London 8 November
Military Odyssey: Kent County Showground, Detling, Maidstone 23–25 August
Nottingham Goose Fair: October (dates unconfirmed; check local press)
Notting Hill Carnival: 24–25 August
'Obby 'Oss Day (May Day): Padstow, 1 May
Ould Lammas Fair: Ballycastle 25–26 August
Reading Festival: Richfield Avenue 22–24 August
RHS Chelsea Flower Show: 20–25 May (RHS members only first two days.)
RHS Flower Show: Tatton Park, Nr Knutsford, Cheshire 16–20 July
RHS Hampton Court Palace Flower Show: 1–6 July (RHS members only first two days.)
RHS Malvern Autumn Show: Three Counties Showground 19–21 September
RHS Malvern Spring Show: Three Counties Showground 8–11 May
Royal International Air Tattoo: RAF Fairford, Gloucestershire 18–21 July
Royal Windsor Horse Show: Home Park, Windsor (dates unconfirmed; check www.rwhs.co.uk)
Shrewsbury Folk Festival: 22–25 August
Shropshire County Horse Show: West Midlands Agricultural Showground, Shrewsbury 17 May
Sidmouth Folk Week: 1–8 August
Trooping the Colour: Horse Guards Parade, London 14 June
Three Choirs Festival: Hereford 26 July–2 August
Three Counties Championship Dog Show: Malvern Showground, Malvern 5–8 June
Three Counties Show: Three Counties Showground, Malvern 13–15 June
Up Helly Aa (fire festival and torchlight parade): Lerwick, Shetland Isles 28 January
Whitby Folk Festival: 23–29 August
Wimbledon Lawn Tennis Championships: 30 June–13 July

In the 328th year of continuous publication

Lighting-up Times for 2025

Vehicle lamps must be used between sunset and sunrise. Times are in GMT, except 01.00 on 30 March to 01.00 on 26 October when they are DST (1 hour in advance). They are calculated for London (longitude 0°, latitude N.51°5).

Day	January h m	February h m	March h m	April h m	May h m	June h m	July h m	August h m	September h m	October h m	November h m	December h m
1	16 32	17 20	18 11	20 04	20 54	21 38	21 50	21 18	20 16	19 07	17 03	16 24
2	16 33	17 22	18 12	20 05	20 55	21 39	21 50	21 16	20 14	19 05	17 01	16 24
3	16 34	17 24	18 14	20 07	20 57	21 40	21 49	21 14	20 11	19 03	16 59	16 23
4	16 35	17 25	18 16	20 09	20 58	21 41	21 49	21 13	20 09	19 01	16 57	16 23
5	16 37	17 27	18 18	20 10	21 00	21 42	21 48	21 11	20 07	18 58	16 56	16 22
6	16 38	17 29	18 19	20 12	21 02	21 43	21 48	21 09	20 05	18 56	16 54	16 22
7	16 39	17 31	18 21	20 14	21 03	21 44	21 47	21 07	20 02	18 54	16 52	16 22
8	16 40	17 33	18 23	20 15	21 05	21 45	21 47	21 05	20 00	18 52	16 51	16 21
9	16 42	17 34	18 25	20 17	21 06	21 45	21 46	21 04	19 58	18 49	16 49	16 21
10	16 43	17 36	18 26	20 19	21 08	21 46	21 45	21 02	19 56	18 47	16 48	16 21
11	16 45	17 38	18 28	20 20	21 10	21 47	21 44	21 00	19 53	18 45	16 46	16 21
12	16 46	17 40	18 30	20 22	21 11	21 47	21 43	20 58	19 51	18 43	16 45	16 21
13	16 48	17 42	18 31	20 24	21 13	21 48	21 43	20 56	19 49	18 41	16 43	16 21
14	16 49	17 44	18 33	20 25	21 14	21 49	21 42	20 54	19 46	18 38	16 42	16 21
15	16 51	17 45	18 35	20 27	21 16	21 49	21 41	20 52	19 44	18 36	16 40	16 21
16	16 52	17 47	18 37	20 29	21 17	21 50	21 40	20 50	19 42	18 34	16 39	16 21
17	16 54	17 49	18 38	20 30	21 19	21 50	21 39	20 48	19 39	18 32	16 38	16 21
18	16 55	17 51	18 40	20 32	21 20	21 50	21 37	20 46	19 37	18 30	16 36	16 22
19	16 57	17 53	18 42	20 34	21 22	21 51	21 36	20 44	19 35	18 28	16 35	16 22
20	16 59	17 55	18 43	20 35	21 23	21 51	21 35	20 42	19 33	18 26	16 34	16 23
21	17 00	17 56	18 45	20 37	21 24	21 51	21 34	20 40	19 30	18 24	16 33	16 23
22	17 02	17 58	18 47	20 39	21 26	21 51	21 32	20 38	19 28	18 22	16 32	16 24
23	17 04	18 00	18 48	20 40	21 27	21 51	21 31	20 36	19 26	18 20	16 31	16 24
24	17 06	18 02	18 50	20 42	21 28	21 51	21 30	20 33	19 23	18 18	16 30	16 25
25	17 07	18 04	18 52	20 44	21 30	21 51	21 28	20 31	19 21	17 16	16 29	16 25
26	17 09	18 05	18 54	20 45	21 31	21 51	21 27	20 29	19 19	17 14	16 28	16 26
27	17 11	18 07	18 55	20 47	21 32	21 51	21 26	20 27	19 16	17 12	16 27	16 27
28	17 12	18 09	18 57	20 49	21 33	21 51	21 24	20 25	19 14	17 10	16 26	16 28
29	17 14		18 59	20 50	21 35	21 51	21 23	20 23	19 12	17 08	16 26	16 29
30	17 16		20 00	20 52	21 36	21 51	21 21	20 20	19 10	17 06	16 25	16 30
31	17 18		20 02		21 37		21 19	20 18		17 04		16 31

Raphael's Astronomical Ephemeris 2025

978-0-572-04847-1

The most reliable astronomical ephemeris you can buy. Available from good bookshops, phone 01256 302699 or from www.foulsham.com

Also available in two Multi-Year Collections

1950–2000

978-0-572-03908-0

2000–2050

978-0-572-03909-7